RALPH BUNCHE

The **African-American Biographies** Series

MAYA ANGELOU
More Than a Poet
0-89490-684-4

LOUIS ARMSTRONG
King of Jazz
0-89490-997-5

ARTHUR ASHE
Breaking the Color
Barrier in Tennis
0-89490-689-5

BENJAMIN BANNEKER
Astronomer and
Mathematician
0-7660-1208-5

RALPH BUNCHE
Winner of the
Nobel Peace Prize
0-7660-1203-4

DUKE ELLINGTON
Giant of Jazz
0-89490-691-7

ARETHA FRANKLIN
Motown Superstar
0-89490-686-0

WHOOPI GOLDBERG
Comedian and Movie Star
0-7660-1205-0

LORRAINE HANSBERRY
Playwright and
Voice of Justice
0-89490-945-2

LANGSTON HUGHES
Poet of the
Harlem Renaissance
0-89490-815-4

ZORA NEALE HURSTON
Southern Storyteller
0-89490-685-2

QUINCY JONES
Musician, Composer,
Producer
0-89490-814-6

BARBARA JORDAN
Congresswoman, Lawyer,
Educator
0-89490-692-5

MARTIN LUTHER KING, JR.
Leader for
Civil Rights
0-89490-687-9

CORETTA SCOTT KING
Striving for
Civil Rights
0-89490-811-1

TONI MORRISON
Nobel Prize-Winning
Author
0-89490-688-7

WALTER DEAN MYERS
Writer for Real Teens
0-7660-1206-9

JESSE OWENS
Track and Field Legend
0-89490-812-X

COLIN POWELL
Soldier and Patriot
0-89490-810-3

PAUL ROBESON
Actor, Singer,
Political Activist
0-89490-944-4

JACKIE ROBINSON
Baseball's Civil Rights
Legend
0-89490-690-9

IDA B. WELLS-BARNETT
Crusader Against Lynching
0-89490-947-9

OPRAH WINFREY
Talk Show Legend
0-7660-1207-7

CARTER G. WOODSON
Father of African-American History
0-89490-946-0

—African-American Biographies—

RALPH BUNCHE

Winner of the Nobel Peace Prize

Series Consultant:
Dr. Russell L. Adams, Chairman
Department of Afro-American Studies, Howard University

Anne Schraff

Enslow Publishers, Inc.

44 Fadem Road   PO Box 38
Box 699   Aldershot
Springfield, NJ 07081 Hants GU12 6BP
USA   UK
http://www.enslow.com

Library of Congress Cataloging-in-Publication Data

Schraff, Anne E.
    Ralph Bunche : winner of the Nobel Peace Prize / by Anne Schraff.
        p. cm. — (African-American biographies)
    Includes bibliographical references and index.
    Summary: Discusses the personal and professional life of the
statesman and diplomat who was one of the founders of the United
Nations and who received the Nobel Prize for his peacemaking efforts.
    ISBN 0-7660-1203-4
    1. Bunche, Ralph J. (Ralph Johnson), 1904–1971—Juvenile
literature. 2. Statesman—United States—Biography—Juvenile
literature. 3. Afro-Americans—Biography—Juvenile literature.
4. United Nations—Biography—Juvenile literature. [1. Bunche,
Ralph J. (Ralph Johnson), 1904–1971. 2. Statesman. 3. Afro-
Americans—Biography. 4. Nobel Prizes—Biography.] I. Title.
II. Series.
E748.B885S37   1999
341.23'3'092—dc21
[B]   98-26886
                                                         CIP
                                                         AC

Printed in the United States of America

10 9 8 7 6 5 4 3 2 1

To Our Readers:
All Internet addresses in this book were active and appropriate when we went
to press. Any comments or suggestions can be sent by e-mail to
Comments@enslow.com or to the address on the back cover.

Illustration Credits: Corel, p. 55; Courtesy Dwight D. Eisenhower
Library, p. 86; Courtesy Richard M. Nixon Library, p. 110; Department
of Special Collections, Charles E. Young Research Library, University of
California at Los Angeles, p. 35; Enslow Publishers, Inc., pp. 60, 61, 114;
George I. Browne, courtesy Franklin Roosevelt Library, p. 82;
Photographs and Prints Division, Schomberg Center for Research in
Black Culture/The New York Public Library/Astor, Lenox and Tilden
Foundations, p. 74; Property of the Lillian P. Benbow Room of Special
Collections, Tougaloo College, Tougaloo, Mississippi, pp. 76, 96, 100;
Reproduced from the Collections of the Library of Congress, p. 6; U.S.
Department of State, courtesy Harry S. Truman Library, p. 102; UN/DPI
photo, pp. 69, 95, 113; United Nations, courtesy Franklin Roosevelt
Library, p. 47; UPI/CORBIS-BETTMANN, pp. 16, 27, 39, 63; Yoichi R.
Okamoto, Lyndon Baines Johnson Library Collection, p. 107;

Cover Illustration: Yoichi R. Okamoto, Lyndon Baines Johnson Library
Collection

CONTENTS

Ralph Bunche

1

ASSASSINATION IN JERUSALEM

he Middle East was a dangerous place in 1948. "We risk our lives out here almost everyday," wrote Ralph Bunche to his wife, Ruth.[1] Ralph Bunche, chief representative of the secretary-general of the United Nations, was in the area then known as Palestine to help bring peace.

A year had passed since the United Nations voted to split Palestine into a Jewish state and an Arab state. The Arabs and Jews both claimed the land, and there was widespread violence between them. In February 1948, fifty-two Jews were killed by an Arab terrorist bomb in Jerusalem. In April, two hundred fifty Arabs died at the hands of Jewish terrorists in an Arab village. In May, the Jewish section of Palestine declared itself to be the State of Israel. The nearby Arab nations did not accept this claim, and they sent their armies into Palestine. The fighting escalated into full-scale war: Israel was at war with several neighboring Arab states.

In June, after weeks of bitter fighting between the Arabs and the Jews, a cease-fire was called. It had been arranged by United Nations–appointed mediator Count Folke Bernadotte of Sweden, assisted by Ralph Bunche. Still, the truce was only temporary. A permanent peace treaty had to be drawn up and signed. Bernadotte and Bunche would be working frantically toward this goal in the summer of 1948.

Relations between the Jews and the Arabs were like a bomb ready to explode. During the truce, both sides were busy stockpiling weapons for the next round of fighting. They gathered tanks, airplanes, and ammunition so they would be ready when shots rang out again.

Bunche wrote to his wife about airplane landings on small, bomb-damaged fields. He described walking through snipers' territory where a single shot from an unseen gunman could end a life.

Bernadotte and Bunche worked nonstop, hurrying between the Arab and the Jewish sectors of Jerusalem for peace talks. Bernadotte often rushed to Cairo for meetings. Both men knew that if they failed to get a peace treaty signed, an even more terrible war would break out.

The headquarters for the United Nations peace team was on the Greek island of Rhodes in the Aegean Sea. The island, located between Greece and Turkey, is less than two hours' flight from Jerusalem. After rounds of meetings with Jewish and Arab leaders, Bernadotte and Bunche would fly back to Rhodes to plan new strategies.

On September 16, 1948, Bernadotte left for Jerusalem while Bunche stayed in Rhodes. Bunche was putting the finishing touches on the 130-page report that he and Bernadotte had written. The report suggested the basis for a permanent peace in the area. The next day Bunche would fly to Jerusalem to meet Bernadotte at his hotel. Then, together, they would try to sell the peace plan to the Arabs and the Jews.

Late in the afternoon of September 17, Bunche landed at Kalandia Airport in Jerusalem. Mechanical trouble had delayed the flight. The passengers had also been slowed down by the red tape involved in entering Israel. With all the delays, there was the possibility that Bernadotte would not wait for Bunche at the hotel.

There were even more delays at the Mandelbaum Gate checkpoint in Jerusalem. As Bunche waited for permission to proceed, an Israeli staff car came speeding up. An officer brought the shocking news that Count Bernadotte had been assassinated.

It seems that Bernadotte had waited thirty minutes for Bunche to arrive at the hotel. When Bunche did not show up, Bernadotte decided to go ahead to the meeting without him. Sitting in the car next to Bernadotte, in the seat usually occupied by Bunche, was Colonel André P. Sérot, a French United Nations official. As they drove through the Katamon Quarter of Jerusalem, a jeep halted Bernadotte's car. Three armed men clad in khaki shorts and shirts approached the car. They were dressed like Israeli soldiers so they would not stand out. The men carried small machine guns. One of them came to the window of Bernadotte's car and fired a volley of shots, killing both Bernadotte and Sérot.

After hearing this news, Ralph Bunche was taken to the nearby YMCA building, where the bodies of Bernadotte and Sérot had been laid out. Bunche believed that if not for all the delays, he, not Sérot, would have been in that seat when bullets ripped into the car. Bunche felt certain that the shot that killed Serot had been meant for him.[2]

The assassination was blamed on a renegade Jewish military group called the Stern Gang. In an interview later, a member of the Stern Gang said that Bernadotte favored making Jerusalem an international city. In fact, this suggestion was in the report Bunche and Bernadotte had written. Stern Gang member Baruch

Nadel believed that if Bernadotte lived, he would have succeeded in removing Jerusalem from Israel. "So we had to kill him on this day," Nadel said.[3]

In the ten days after the assassination, Bunche worked day and night to keep the peace effort going. He said he was "completely exhausted but not shattered."[4] On September 20, 1948, the United Nations Security Council named Ralph Bunche as acting mediator, replacing Bernadotte. Now the burden of finding a peaceful solution to the Palestine crisis was entirely on Bunche's shoulders. Would the peace talks come to a complete standstill without Bernadotte? Could Bunche succeed in the leadership role in this struggle for peace?

When Bunche took over the job of mediator, he was well aware of the dangers he faced. Ruth Bunche, alarmed by the worsening situation, pleaded in a letter to her husband, "Please be careful."[5] Six United Nations officials, including Bernadotte, had been killed. Seven United Nations observers had been wounded. Bullet holes riddled many United Nations vehicles in the Middle East. It was the first time Ralph Bunche was risking his life for peace, but it would not be the last.

2

THE LONG
JOURNEY WEST

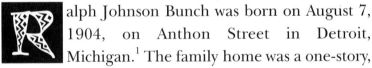alph Johnson Bunch was born on August 7,
1904, on Anthon Street in Detroit,
Michigan.[1] The family home was a one-story,
white frame house with green shutters and a large
front porch. It was located about a mile from the
Detroit River. (The spelling of the family name—
Bunch—was changed to *Bunche* about fourteen years
later when Ralph's maternal grandmother, Lucy
Johnson, added the *e* to give her two grandchildren a
fresh start in life.)

Ralph's grandfather was Thomas Nelson Johnson,
a dedicated teacher in Kansas and Texas. When he

died, Lucy Johnson was only thirty-five years old. She was left to support five children by herself. She and her children moved to Alton, Illinois, on the shores of Lake Michigan. There, Lucy Johnson managed to keep her family fed, clothed, and housed by working at house-keeping and factory jobs. Later, they moved back to Anthon Street in Detroit.

One of her five children was Olive Agnes Johnson, Ralph's mother. A beautiful girl with dark, smiling eyes, Olive helped care for her four brothers and sisters while their mother worked.

One day at a baseball game, Olive Johnson met a young barber from Zanesville, Ohio. Fred Bunch was handsome, with smooth olive skin and bright, dark eyes. Bunch was traveling with a circus. When the circus set up tents in a new city, Bunch cut hair and was a barker as well. (A barker announces the attractions at the circus.) Johnson and Bunch fell in love and were married. Fred Bunch did not have much money, so the young couple moved in with the Johnson family in the small house on Anthon Street.

Fred Bunch was a good barber, but he was never very successful. A friend of the family called him a "lovable carefree chap who couldn't sit still."[2] Bunch charged ten cents for a haircut and five cents for a shave, but few customers came. It was a poor neighborhood, and most men could not afford a barber. Instead, family members cut each other's hair. Few men could afford the luxury of a shave at the barbershop. Money troubles dogged the Bunch family, and they moved often as Fred Bunch looked for jobs.

Between 1907 and 1909, the Bunch family lived in three cities: Cleveland, Ohio; Knoxville, Tennessee; and Toledo, Ohio. In Toledo, young Ralph attended Barstow School. He sold newspapers on street corners to add to the family income. Ralph's sister, Grace, was born in 1909. By then Olive Bunch was sick with a lingering cough. Fred Bunch was out of work again and the family lived in one room.

On a visit to Toledo, Lucy Johnson, Ralph's grandmother, who was known as Nana, found the family beset by poverty and illness. She took them back to Detroit and supported them there. Nana cleaned houses, ironed, tended neighbors' children, and mowed lawns to earn money. Fred Bunch often had to travel out of town to find any work. When Olive Bunch's cough was found to be caused by tuberculosis, a serious and contagious lung disease, she was sent away to a sanitarium. During this time Nana cared for Ralph and Grace.

When the Bunch family was together, there was often music. Ralph Bunche later recalled: "My childhood days were poor days, but happy ones and filled with music."[3] The family always had a piano, and when Olive Bunch was well, she led the family in singing. Olive joined her brothers and sisters in a group called

Ralph Bunche, age four. Ralph's family was very poor, and they moved from city to city as his father looked for work.

the Johnson Quartette. They performed around Detroit.

When he was grown, Ralph Bunche often remembered a special afternoon he spent with his mother. They were watching the sunset together when she said, "My boy, don't ever let anything take away your hope and faith and dreams."[4] Bunche said that he never forgot those words, and "they have served me well."[5]

As a youngster, Ralph enjoyed sledding in the winter. He would tie his sled to the tailgate of horse-drawn wagons and go gliding through the snow. In the summer, Ralph and his friends swam at Belle Isle and in the river near the icehouse in Detroit. Ralph loved the circus. When the Barnum and Bailey Circus came to town, he always went. He enjoyed baseball, too, and was a big Detroit Tigers fan. Ralph made friends with the players. He handed them their bats and was allowed to sit in the Tigers' dugout.

Ralph played "shinny," a type of street hockey with tin cans for pucks and branches for sticks. He used tobacco sacks for baseballs. He often skated and rode his scooter down the streets of Detroit.

In September 1914, Lucy Johnson decided the family should move west to Albuquerque, New Mexico. At that time it was a popular health resort for people with lung trouble. Nana hoped that the clean, dry mountain air would help her daughter Olive regain her health.

The Bunch family found a small adobe house on Fifth Street in Albuquerque. A neighbor described Olive Bunch as "so gentle and good" and "about as near an angel as anyone I would ever see."[6] At first, Olive Bunch felt better there. She enjoyed going to band concerts in the park.

Young Ralph went hunting on the mesas for quail and cottontail rabbits. Nana cooked wonderful feasts of stewed chicken, dumplings, baked apples, and biscuits. Ralph made many friends among the Mexican and American Indian children in the neighborhood.

Still, family life at the Bunch house was always overshadowed by Olive Bunch's poor health. She rested for most of the day and her steps were growing unsteady. Fred Bunch had to leave Albuquerque to find work. To earn money for his family, Ralph helped salesmen carry their luggage from the train station to nearby hotels. As always, Nana worked hard to keep the family afloat. But nobody could do anything to prevent the tragedy about to strike.

In February 1917, thirty-five-year-old Olive Bunch died of tuberculosis. Eight-year-old Grace wept at her mother's grave and thirteen-year-old Ralph put his arm around Grace to comfort her. Later, Ralph Bunche would remember his mother as a "pretty, very sweet and romantic lady, a dreamer."[7]

After his wife's death, Fred Bunch drifted around the country seeking work. Ralph never saw his father again, but he treasured a gift his father had once given him—a tiepin. It remained a precious memento from a father crushed by his troubles.

During his years in Albuquerque, Ralph had a very special teacher, Miss Emma Belle Sweet, at the fourth ward elementary school. When Ralph entered sixth grade, he was one of only two African-American children in a class of sixty-five students. Sweet was strict, but she treated everyone fairly and equally. In Sweet's class, Ralph overcame his shyness. Although he earned high grades in the academic subjects, he was marked down in behavior because he talked too much and sometimes threw spitballs.

Many years later, when Ralph Bunche received the National Education Association's Gold Key Award, he said that Sweet had a great influence on his life. He nominated her for the most influential teacher award, for which she received $1,000. Bunche said of Sweet, "I have never met a nicer lady nor one more appropriately named."[8]

With Olive Bunch dead, and Fred Bunch gone, Nana saw no reason to remain in Albuquerque. Los Angeles beckoned, with its excellent climate and many opportunities for young people like Ralph and Grace. In 1917, Nana and the Bunch children moved to Los Angeles. For their new start, they got an *e* at the end of their last name and a home on Thirty-seventh Street in a white, middle-class neighborhood. (Today this neighborhood is called Watts and has a mostly African-American population.)

Ralph Bunche always noted how much strength he received from his grandmother. He remembered her saying, "Our family is fine as any on earth. We are poor in money, all right, but we're all rich in character, spirit, and decency and we believe in God. That's a lot more important than money—or color."[9] Ralph's grandmother served as his main parent for much of his childhood, and she filled that role well. "She was small—almost tiny," Bunche later said, "soft spoken and shy. But she was strong, very strong in character, will and spirit."[10]

One time, right after Nana and the Bunches moved to Los Angeles, a cemetery plot salesman came to the door of their house. Ralph's grandmother was light-skinned and was often mistaken for a white person. The salesman, who thought she was white, told her that she could rest assured no African Americans or Mexican Americans would be buried nearby. Nana chased the man from her home with a broom.

In 1917, Ralph entered Thirtieth Street Intermediate School (now John Adams Junior High). The school counselors placed him in vocational classes. They assumed that an African American would not be preparing for college, but instead would need skills to help land a job right after high school. Ralph was enrolled in shorthand and commercial arithmetic.

Ralph's grandmother would have none of this. She demanded that Ralph be transferred to a college-preparatory track. He did very well in the more demanding classes.

Ralph went on to Jefferson High School, which was a half block away from his home. At this school he strongly felt the sting of racial prejudice. There had been minor incidents before. At age six he had been with his mother on a train in Knoxville, Tennessee, when they were ordered to the "colored" section of the train. Olive Bunch refused to move and the conductor gave in. But now, at Jefferson High School, Ralph was refused admittance to the citywide honor society—the Ephebian Society—because of his race. He had the grades to qualify, but his color kept him out. Ralph was so angry he almost quit school, but he recalled his mother's advice not to let anyone take his dreams away, and he stayed.

Another painful incident of racial prejudice happened when Ralph worked as a delivery boy for the *Los Angeles Times* newspaper. He was also a "pig boy," someone who worked at the printing plant carrying lead bricks to the typesetting machines. There was a close camaraderie among the pig boys. One day the *Times* arranged an outing for all of them at the Venice Plunge, a public swimming pool. As the other boys jumped into the cool, inviting water, Ralph was stopped and told "whites only." He had to sit on a bench and listen to the happy shouts of his companions as they splashed in the pool. Later, Ralph Bunche described those "whites only" signs as an "insolent mockery" of the black race.[11]

Ralph graduated from Jefferson High School in 1922 with high honors. He was the class valedictorian: the student with the highest grades in the senior class. Meaning to compliment Ralph, the principal told Ralph's grandmother that he never thought of Ralph as a Negro. Ralph's grandmother quickly said, "He is a Negro, and proud of it."[12]

During the summer after graduation, Ralph learned carpet laying at the City Dye Works. He was making more money now, and he enjoyed spending it. He and his friends partied and raced up and down Central Avenue in their cars. His education could have stopped right there. He was a fun-loving, high-spirited young man, and an exciting world called to him. But Ralph's grandmother insisted that he go on to college. She talked about it endlessly until Ralph finally agreed. He enrolled at the University of California at Los Angeles (UCLA) in 1922. Later he admitted that it never would have happened except for his grandmother's insistence. He did not have the heart to dash her high hopes for his future.

3

SCHOLAR-ATHLETE

It was his grandmother's idea that he go to college, but Ralph Bunche quickly learned to love it. Bunche had a well-rounded life at UCLA and enthusiastically took part in academics as well as athletic and social activities. He was a writer for the UCLA newspaper, the *Daily Bruin*. He edited the sports edition of the college yearbook. To help afford the cost of college, Bunche saved money by living at home and working many jobs. His first job was trimming the ivy on the old college buildings on the Vermont Street campus. Bunche worked as a houseboy for silent-screen star Charlie Ray.

Bunche spent a summer session of the Reserve Officers Training Corps (ROTC) at Camp Lewis in Washington state. On his trip home from ROTC camp, he tried to save money by stowing away on the Admiral liner *H. F. Alexander.* Young Bunche was discovered aboard the ship and sent to the galley to work off his fare as a messman—a kitchen helper. He was so good at this job that he was hired to work on the ship for the next three summers.

From his various jobs, Bunche saved money to buy a Model T Ford. He and a friend used it to set up their own business cleaning stores and luncheonettes in the neighborhood. Bunche managed to pay his college expenses and help out at home, but he could not save any money.

Despite many hours spent working, Bunche also had fun at college. His warm personality attracted many friends on the mostly white campus. Bunche loved parties and he was invited to many. A favorite activity was picnicking on the nearby beaches with his college friends.

Ralph Bunche was not a great athlete, but he was good and he had spirit. He played football and basketball at UCLA. Later he recalled that he believed his greatest contribution to one important basketball game was running up and down the court shouting, "We can beat these boys!"[1] In fact, Bunche's team did beat the stronger team. His basketball coach described Bunche as "a versatile young man of limitless energy."[2]

Unfortunately, during his years as an athlete at UCLA, Bunche first suffered two serious physical problems that would continue to give him difficulties for the rest of his life. As a freshman, Bunche began getting severe headaches. He was studying and working hard, so he blamed his headaches on his rigorous schedule. But when the headaches kept getting worse, he went to a doctor. A piece of barley straw was found imbedded in his left ear. Nobody knew how it got there, but it probably had happened on a windy day. The ear was infected, and that was causing the headaches. An operation to eliminate the infection in the mastoid bone failed. (The mastoid is the large cone-shaped bone behind the ear. An infection here is serious because it is so close to the brain.) A second operation solved the problem but left Bunche deaf in his left ear.

The second physical problem was a football injury that caused a blood clot in Bunche's left calf. His leg had to be tightly bandaged with cotton gauze. The injury forced Bunche to give up football. He then put all his energy into basketball. But basketball was also hard on his legs. Running and jumping on the basketball court further damaged the veins. As a result, many years later Bunche would have difficulty walking.

Bunche continued to play basketball, and he

helped the UCLA team, the Bruins, win the Southern Conference basketball championship three years in a row. Each member of the team was given a golden basketball for each winning year. Bunche treasured his three golden basketballs all his life. Many years later, when Bunche's house was robbed, he was greatly relieved to learn that his golden basketballs were safe.[3]

Bunche was an excellent student and a fine public speaker. However, he was not welcome to join the UCLA debating team because of his race. Bunche and his friends fought back by starting their own debating club—the Southern Branch Debating Society. Bunche was immediately elected president. In one major oratorical contest, Bunche opened with his favorite biblical quote from Isaiah about men beating their swords into plowshares and making war no more. Even at this young age, Bunche held the cause of peace in his heart.

At UCLA, Bunche majored in political science. He was elected to Phi Beta Kappa, the most prestigious honor society in the United States. It is open only to the very best students. In 1927, Bunche graduated from UCLA summa cum laude, which means "with highest honors." He was the top student in his class and became valedictorian. In his speech at the graduation ceremony, he asked his fellow students to work for the cause of peace.

Because Bunche was an exceptionally brilliant scholar, he was given a fellowship to Harvard University

At the University of California at Los Angeles, Ralph Bunche was a spirited athlete. His basketball coach called him a player with "limitless energy."

after he graduated from UCLA. The fellowship covered tuition for graduate study but not books or living expenses at the Cambridge, Massachusetts, campus. Bunche did not have the money to accept this great opportunity, so his friends and family pitched in to help. Bunche's uncle Tom Johnson and his aunt Nelle helped out by giving musical concerts at churches. A group of local African-American women—the Friday Morning Club of Los Angeles—also gave concerts and teas to raise money for Bunche. They raised $1,000, and Bunche's relatives raised additional money. So Bunche was able to go to Harvard University after all.

When Ralph Bunche arrived at Harvard, he was among about forty African-American students out of a total enrollment of about two thousand students. As he had done at UCLA, Bunche quickly made friends. One of his close friends was fellow African American Robert Weaver, who later became an economist. Weaver later recalled Bunche from their student days at Harvard, calling him "extremely attractive, quite vocal, articulate and approachable." Weaver said Bunche had "a well developed sense of humor" with the special gift of being able "to laugh at himself."[4]

To earn expense money, Bunche worked at John Phillips's secondhand bookstore in Harvard Square. Bunche was a good student at Harvard. In June 1928, he received a master of arts degree in political science. He was immediately offered a position at Howard

University, a highly respected African-American college in Washington, D.C. Though he was only twenty-five years old, Bunche was asked to teach at Howard and to set up a political science department.

At Howard University, Bunche was a fine teacher. He also spoke up on behalf of his students. A group of his students picketed a Washington restaurant that did not serve nonwhite customers alongside whites. Bunche helped lead the student battle against segregation. He refused to accept racial injustice.

Bunche's years at Howard were not spent just in the classroom. While there, he met the most important person in his adult life: Ruth Ethel Harris. She was an elementary-school teacher who was taking night classes at Howard University to earn a bachelor's degree. One day in October 1928, Harris and some friends invited several young men from Howard to a get-together at her home. Bunche had already noticed Harris. He told his friends that he planned to ask "that quiet little girl" by the piano bench for a date.[5] Bunche did just that, and the couple began dating.

Ruth Harris was from Montgomery, Alabama. Her father, Charles Oscar Harris, was a graduate of Howard University. He had been chief mailing clerk at the Montgomery Post Office for thirty-five years. Ruth was one of ten children, and her parents used up all their resources so their children would have a good education. When the family moved to Washington, D.C., Ruth Harris enrolled at Howard University.

Bunche had to return to Harvard in the fall of 1929 to complete preliminary course work for his doctorate. It was a stressful year for both Bunche and Harris. Bunche was shouldering a heavy academic schedule, and he and Harris were missing each other. They wrote letters to each other almost every day.

On June 23, 1930, Ralph Bunche married Ruth Harris at her brother's home in Washington, D.C. Until two months before the wedding, Bunche did not even know how he and his new bride would live during the upcoming summer. Until school began in September, he would have no money. They figured they would need about $700 to see them through the summer. That would pay for their room in a boarding-house and cover the down payment on a car. Then came a happy surprise. Bunche was awarded a scholarship that provided just what the couple needed. They rushed right out to buy the car of their dreams—a blue Ford coupe with a rumble seat in the back. They were able to make the down payment on the $619 automobile, keep up the payments, and pay Ma Clark $40 a month for their room in her boardinghouse. The Bunches were off to a good start.

4

AFRICAN ROOTS

R alph Bunche worked at Howard University from 1928 to 1933. He continued as a political science professor there until 1950 on a part-time basis. Bunche was a tireless and devoted teacher in spite of many health problems. Though he was only in his late twenties and early thirties, he was dogged by headaches, indigestion, colds, and toothaches. He had his tonsils removed, hoping to prevent the colds. He received a serum injection for the blood clot in his leg from the old football injury at UCLA. Despite his health problems, Bunche took on an ever-increasing workload.

During the early 1930s, Ralph Bunche wrote many magazine articles and gave many speeches. In one article he tried to advance African-American political power by analyzing the black vote in Chicago.[1] By this time, Bunche was a bright young scholar much in demand. He was becoming famous. Bunche's doctoral dissertation was titled "French Administration in Togoland and Dahomey." Both of these colonies in Africa were ruled by the French, but Togoland was also managed as a mandate territory under the League of Nations. Both Dahomey (now Benim) and Togoland (now Togo) later became independent countries. Bunche wanted to find out whether the involvement of the League of Nations made a difference in how the people were treated.

In 1929, the stock market crashed and the United States was plunged into a deep economic depression. Millions of people were out of work, and families lost their homes. Many farms were auctioned off because farmers could not afford mortgage payments. There was even widespread hunger in some parts of the country.

The Bunche family was not directly affected by the Great Depression. Ralph Bunche continued to work at Howard University, but he was aware of the sufferings of fellow Americans. In fact, the Depression was especially hard on African Americans, who had very little to begin with. Even in normal economic times, African

Americans were at the bottom of the barrel, but during the Depression, with the entire barrel sinking, they were truly in desperate straits.

In 1931, Bunche received a Rosenwald Fellowship to spend the 1931–32 academic year in Europe and Africa to study Togoland and Dahomey. The fellowship was awarded to outstanding young African Americans by Julius Rosenwald, builder of the Sears, Roebuck Company. Bunche delayed leaving on this journey because his wife was expecting their first child. He wanted to be at her side for the birth and planned to spend time with his family for a while after.

Joan Bunche was born in December 1931. Bunche completed his research, then sailed to Europe on June 15, 1932. He went tourist class on the ship *Europa*. The fellowship was quite a windfall for the struggling young family. In addition to his $2,000 annual salary as a Howard University professor, he would earn $2,500 on the fellowship. This was a lot of money at that time, especially for an African American.

When Bunche arrived in Paris, he immediately missed his family. He cabled Ruth and asked her to come with their baby daughter as soon as she could. Ruth arrived in Paris in July with baby Joan in her arms.

The Bunches spent several months in Paris while Ralph Bunche did research to prepare for his trip to Africa. Bunche left for Africa in November 1932, and his family remained in Paris. He spent about three months traveling in Dahomey and Togoland and doing research on the governments. He visited the ruins of royal palaces from ancient Dahomey. The Dahomey civilization flourished in the seventeenth and eighteenth centuries until France defeated the last of the Dahomey kings in 1894.

Bunche concluded that there was little difference in how Dahomey and Togoland were governed.[2] He wrote his report and rejoined his family in Paris in January 1933. The Bunches returned to the United States. Their second daughter, Jane, was born in May.

Ralph Bunche was off to Cambridge, England, for the summer of 1933 to put the finishing touches on his doctoral dissertation. It was 450 pages long. In February 1934, Bunche was awarded his Ph.D. from Harvard University. He was the first African American to receive a doctorate in political science.

Bunche believed that real equality was linked to economic and political change. He studied the measures being taken to move the United States out of the Depression by the new president, Franklin Roosevelt. This program, called the New Deal, set up long-range economic reforms and emergency welfare agencies to help the needy. When progress did not take place as fast as Bunche hoped, especially for African Americans, he was disappointed in the New Deal.[3] In

Over the years, Bunche studied in many African nations and met
many African leaders.

1935, Bunche said, "For the Negro population, the New Deal means the same thing but more of it."[4]

That year, the National Negro Congress (NNC), a coalition of blacks and whites in support of black workers, was formed. Bunche hoped this group would help African Americans make real progress in reaching the American dream of a good life.

At the 1936 NNC convention in Chicago, Bunche was among the eight hundred delegates representing civil rights organizations, church groups, fraternities, and trade unions. In later years, when he noticed Communist influence on the organization, he withdrew.[5]

By July 1936, Ruth Bunche was growing unhappy about her husband's many absences. He never seemed to be home. His research was frequently taking him to Europe and Africa. "I want you to have everything good," Ruth Bunche wrote her husband, "and all the success in the world, but I do hate to see our family break up."[6] At the time, Ruth was teaching first grade and caring for their two daughters. The family lived with her mother, who watched the children during the day. Ruth Bunche took over their care when she got home in the afternoon. Both of the Bunche daughters were under four years of age, and Ruth Bunche missed her husband's help in bringing up the spirited little girls.

In January 1937, Ralph Bunche asked his wife to join him on a trip to Europe. When she agreed to come with the children, he was delighted.[7] The whole family sailed for Europe on the *Berengaria*, docking in England. Ralph Bunche was based at the London School of Economics. Here he took seminars with many famous people, including Jomo Kenyatta, a Kikuyu tribe member who later became the founding president of Kenya. Bunche met many rising young African leaders from the Gold Coast (now Ghana) and from Uganda.

Paul Robeson, the world-famous African-American actor and singer, was living in London then. Robeson was an activist against racial prejudice, and he and the Bunches became friends. The Bunche home in London became a meeting place for many prominent people. Some held pro-Communist views, and they urged Bunche to join the Communist Party, but he refused. While in London, Ralph Bunche visited Parliament to watch lively debates between Lloyd George, a former prime minister, and Clement Attlee, who would become prime minister in 1945.

The year 1937 was an exciting and joyful time for the Bunche family. Bunche noted that the family was happier and closer together than it had been.[8] Joan and Jane Bunche went to school at the Froebel Institute and enjoyed it. A generous neighbor often baby-sat for the girls in the evenings so Ralph and Ruth Bunche could do what they both loved—go to movies, plays, and dinner parties. It was the first time since 1932 that they had a chance to lead a normal family life for a prolonged period.

The Bunches visited Holland and spent Ralph's thirty-fourth birthday in Brussels, Belgium. Then they spent three weeks in Paris before Ruth Bunche and the girls returned to the United States. Ralph Bunche went alone to Africa. It was a painful parting at the dock at Cherbourg, France. For an hour, Ralph Bunche stood watching the ocean liner as his family boarded, shouting good-byes until the ship moved across the English Channel and out of sight.

Bunche's first book, *A World View of Race*, was published in the United States in 1936. It was a sociological study of race relations in the United States and elsewhere. That same year, Bunche sailed to Capetown, South Africa, for a firsthand look at race relations there.

Upon entering South Africa, Bunche had to find nightly accommodations in nonwhite households because of strict racial separation. (In 1948, the racial separation policies, which had long been in force, were codified in the apartheid laws.) In South Africa there were three major population groups. At the top, with the most privileges, were the whites, who ran the country. In the middle were the "coloured"—people of mixed race. With his fair skin, Bunche resembled a coloured person. At the bottom, with few privileges,

Ralph Bunche's work often took him far from home, and he treasured the time spent with his wife and two daughters, Jane, left, and Joan.

were the black Africans. Commenting on this situation, Bunche said, "I've been knocking around in South Africa trying to find out what sort of magic is employed to enable that handful of very ordinary pale-faces to keep the millions of black and colored so ruthlessly under the thumb."[9]

During his time in South Africa, Bunche kept a detailed diary. He noted that black South Africans had a very high opinion of American black people. African Americans like Bunche were seen as an example of what black people could accomplish if they were free. In the eyes of the black South African, America was a "mecca and oasis."[10]

Recalling his friendship with Jomo Kenyatta in London, Bunche visited a Kikuyu village a few miles from Nairobi in East Africa. The Kikuyu tribe gave Bunche a tribal name, "Karioki," which means "he who has returned from the dead." Bunche had brought along records of famous African-American artists like Paul Robeson, Fats Waller, and Josephine Baker. The Kikuyu village came alive with the majestic sound of Robeson's voice and the songs of Baker and Waller.[11]

Ralph Bunche then embarked on a tour of the backcountry of South Africa. He rode in an old Ford station wagon. The rough clay roads often turned muddy and impassable after a rain. There were long delays as Bunche, his driver, and the cook had to dig the car out of the mud. It was a miserable trip. The food was bad, and sleeping arrangements were little more than stretching out in the station wagon or on the ground. Insects were on the attack, and Bunche was taking quinine for headaches and cramps. During the day, everybody suffered from the intense heat, and the nights were uncomfortably cold.

Bunche stopped at the excavation camp run by Dr. Louis Leakey, the famous British paleontologist who found important human fossils in Africa. Then Bunche went on to the Congo and Uganda. He spent nights in the station wagon while mosquitoes buzzed beyond the windows. It was an exciting but harrowing adventure. It was important to Bunche because it gave him a real feeling for his own African-American roots. It also showed him that racial prejudice was not a uniquely American problem. He saw examples of racial prejudice all over Africa, wherever European nations had colonies.

In April 1938, Bunche went to the Far East, visiting Singapore, Bali, Hong Kong, and Manila. By this time he was worn out from his journeying, and he missed his family. Bunche had been traveling through Africa and Asia from September 1937 to July 1938. Back home in Washington, D.C., Ruth Bunche had been coping with two small children, her job, and the loneliness she frequently mentioned in letters to her husband. She lamented that in their first five years of marriage he had been gone half the time.

Bunche arrived back in the United States on July 7, 1938. Ruth Bunche and the girls flew to Los Angeles three days later to join him. The family enjoyed a vacation together, and they made plans not to be separated so much in the future. For the next six years Ralph Bunche would be with his family. At last, Ruth Bunche would have the kind of life she dreamed of—father and mother working together to raise the children, and husband and wife being there for each other. But as the Bunches settled into ordinary family life, the dark clouds of war gathered in Europe. In time the storm would engulf the United States as well.

5

Sociology and War

While he was in Europe and Africa, Ralph Bunche was named a full professor at Howard University. His income and prestige increased. But after so much adventure around the world, settling down to routine teaching was hard. Teaching American government and constitutional law was not quite like spending the night watching a pride of lions in Africa. Bunche told friends it was a real effort to get back to teaching.[1]

In the summer of 1939, Bunche began working with Gunnar Myrdal, the Swedish sociologist and economist. Myrdal was conducting a massive study on black-white relations in the United States. Myrdal's goal was to produce a fair and unbiased study of the African American in the United States.[2]

Ralph Bunche interviewed African Americans in all walks of life. He asked them how they felt about their lives, and about their hopes and dreams. He asked how they viewed white Americans. Then Bunche wrote long monographs for Myrdal based on the interviews. Bunche said that he hoped the Myrdal report would be "helpful to the Negro in his struggle for equality."[3]

Traveling around the United States with Myrdal was an adventure in itself for Bunche. Bunche was soft-spoken and diplomatic in his interviews. Myrdal was outspoken and aggressive. When Myrdal met white people he believed to be prejudiced, he would bait them and then insult them. Myrdal's daughter, Sissela Bok, later recalled how her father needled people with his "mercilessly irreverent joking."[4] Sometimes Myrdal's hostile behavior put the two men in risky situations. He once interviewed a young white woman in Georgia who was very bigoted against African Americans. In response, he insulted her with sharp humor. The woman was so angry that she swore out a complaint, and a warrant was issued for Myrdal's arrest. Lawyers urged Myrdal and Bunche to leave Georgia at once. Bunche and Myrdal hurriedly moved on to other southern states.

It was hard for Bunche to find places to spend the night. Myrdal could easily book a room in a hotel, but because of his race, Bunche could not get hotel accommodations in many small towns. Bunche usually found a room with a local African-American family. Bunche later remembered that one particular night when he was searching for a place to stay, "the Klan [Ku Klux Klan—an antiblack terrorist group] was riding and no Negro would dare open his shutters."[5] Bunche finally found an African-American mortuary that would take him in. He spent the night sleeping on a slab where a coffin usually rested. In fact, only a screen separated Bunche from the adjacent slab, where a body awaited burial.[6]

Bunche worked feverishly on the work Myrdal assigned him. He was always scrambling to meet deadlines. Bunche eventually produced three thousand pages for the Myrdal report. Still, he lamented that the work had been done too quickly. He feared he had not met his own high standards of scholarship. But, "since there was so little research at all in this field," Bunche said, "it would still be valuable."[7]

Bunche and Myrdal's research eventually became a huge book, *The American Dilemma*, published in 1944. Historian Walter Jackson said that the book fulfilled Bunche's hopes by "helping create a new racial liberalism that influenced political leaders, judges, civil rights activists and thousands of educated white Americans."[8]

In the late 1930s, the rapid rise of fascism (dictatorships) in Europe seemed to be a major threat to world democracy. Adolf Hitler, the dictator of Nazi Germany, believed in the superiority of what he believed was the superrace—his own countrymen. To achieve his goals, he caused death and destruction as no one in modern history had done before. He ordered the imprisonment and murder of tens of thousands of people, including blacks and Communists. Hitler's extermination forces killed six million European Jews and about five million other people considered by Hitler to be racially inferior.[9]

Because of this racial hatred, Bunche saw Hitler's ideas as especially dangerous to dark-skinned people. Bunche said the triumph of Hitler's views would "mean the end of me and my people."[10] Bunche realized that inequality in America discouraged many African Americans from getting involved in the war effort. He spread the word that the crusade to stop Hitler was as much the black citizens' cause as it was the white citizens'.

Bunche wanted to get personally involved in the war effort, so in 1941 he asked for a meeting with First Lady Eleanor Roosevelt. President Franklin D. Roosevelt's wife had been instrumental in advancing the civil rights of African Americans. Eleanor Roosevelt invited Bunche to the White House, and Bunche immediately liked her. He described her as a "very intelligent woman."[11] She had great respect for Bunche, too.[12] They discussed ways of getting African Americans involved in the war effort. Bunche wanted to stress the fact that even though racism was still widespread in the United States, the only hope for everyone's future was the defeat of Hitler. "The fight is to maintain those conditions under which people may

Eleanor Roosevelt, wife of President Franklin D. Roosevelt, was known as an activist for civil rights. She and Ralph Bunche discussed ways to get African Americans involved in the fight against Adolf Hitler in World War II.

continue to strive for realization of the democratic ideals,"[13] Bunche said.

Bunche's college friend Robert Weaver now worked for the Roosevelt administration. He suggested Bunche as a member of a new federal agency, the Office of Coordinator of Information (COI). The COI brought together scholars and journalists to compile and send out information about the war. The aim was to win American public opinion to the cause of fighting Hitler and fascism. Bunche and the others tried to make it clear that Hitler's defeat was very important. At this time Great Britain, France, and other democratic nations were desperately battling Hitler, but the United States had not yet declared war. Some Americans believed the United States should not get involved at all.

The COI was part of the Office of Strategic Services (OSS), which later became the Central Intelligence Agency (CIA). Bunche had now entered the world of government service. Before this, all his work experience had been in education and research. In September 1941, at age thirty-nine, Bunche became a senior social science analyst at COI. His salary was $4,600 a year.

A few months later, on December 7, 1941, Adolf Hitler's Japanese allies attacked the United States naval base at Pearl Harbor in Hawaii. The United States was now at war against the Axis powers—Germany, Japan, and Italy. There was no more doubt now in anybody's mind that this was America's cause, too.

Bunche focused on his area of expertise—Africa. He worked diligently on a pair of manuals for American troops who would be fighting in Africa, *A Guide to North Africa* and *A Guide to West Africa*. Both gave an overview of the culture of the regions, and the military found the guides very helpful. Secretary of State Edward Stettinius wrote to Bunche that "the men who fought in Africa have expressed their great appreciation of your work in grooming them for their job."[14]

While Bunche sold the war effort to the African-American community, his own daughters had to attend segregated all-black schools. In Washington, D.C., blacks could not find equality in the white world. They were barred from restaurants, nightclubs, taxis, city parks, and playgrounds. "Living in the nation's capital is like serving out a sentence," Bunche said. "It's extremely difficult for a Negro to maintain even a semblance of dignity in Washington."[15]

Still, Bunche threw his heart and soul into his federal job. He felt so passionately about the war effort that he wanted to be in uniform himself, but his physical examination at Walter Reed Hospital ended those hopes quickly. He suffered from serious circulatory problems, and he was deaf in one ear. So Bunche put all his efforts into his civilian job.

Bunche worked to increase the number of African Americans in the war industries. He wanted the jobs to be filled on an equitable basis. Bunche helped develop public-service films showing the important contributions African Americans had already made to the United States.

Although Ralph Bunche was working very hard to help his country win World War II, his personal life was not suffering. The job at COI did not demand travel, so Bunche could be home with his family. The Bunches once more enjoyed routine family pleasures. They could go out socially on weekends. Before this, Ruth Bunche was alone so much of the time that she said she sometimes felt like a widow.[16]

In 1941, the Bunches bought their first home, at 1510 Jackson Street N.E., adding to their joy. Now there was even a chance to work in a garden.

On September 18, 1943, the Bunches welcomed their third child, Ralph Jr. Ralph Bunche took a two-week leave of absence from his job. He eagerly entered into the chores of a new father. He described himself as busily "nurse-maiding, sterilizing bottles, [and] making formulae" for his new son.[17]

As a public servant, Bunche showed the same excellent qualities he had shown as an educator. Longtime friend Kenneth Clark said of Bunche, "I never did see any difference between Ralph Bunche, the person, the human being, and Ralph Bunche the public figure, the statesman. . . . He was incapable of flamboyance, even temporary egoism and posturing."[18]

In January 1944, Bunche was sworn in as an officer in the State Department. When World War II came to an end, Bunche could take pride in how much he had contributed to that victory. Now Bunche's career was about to take another dramatic turn. He would step upon a much larger stage.

6

PEACE AT
LAST

n July 1944, Ralph Bunche joined a group of
diplomats dealing with the business of the
old League of Nations. The League of
Nations was an international organization established
after World War I to promote world peace. One of its
activities was helping to prepare Africa and other
colonies for eventual self-rule. Since Bunche was an
expert on Africa from his research and travel, he was
assigned to a committee on African colonies.

In February 1945, world leaders were planning for
a new organization—the United Nations (UN)—to
replace the League of Nations. They hoped this new

organization would be more successful than the League of Nations in preventing future wars. When the other nations of the world sent diplomats to write the charter of the United Nations, Ralph Bunche represented the United States.[1] Bunche was proud to take his place among the delegates of the fifty founding nations of the United Nations. The diplomats met in the San Francisco Opera House and began a tremendous job. Bunche's days were filled with attending meetings, writing papers, and keeping records. His main focus was the fate of African colonies. The goal of the United Nations was that eventually all the colonies of the world would be set on the road to independence.

The San Francisco United Nations conference was a landmark in Bunche's career. He became a respected world diplomat. When Bunche was in college, he had considered a career as an international diplomat. Now that youthful dream was coming true.

While Bunche's career was rising to new heights, problems arose at home. Ruth Bunche had borne the major burden of raising the children during Ralph Bunche's many absences. In addition to this, both Bunches were very strict with their daughters, and now Ralph Bunche worried that as parents they were perhaps too strict. He now resolved to be the same loving person at home that he was at work.[2]

Ralph Bunche's life was totally centered on work and family. He had strong ideas of what an ideal family

Ralph Bunche was among the diplomats invited to write the charter of the new United Nations in 1945.

should be. He wanted his wife to be very supportive, and he wanted his children to do their best in school. Ralph Bunche conducted his own life with strong integrity, and he was always completely loyal to his wife. Even though he was an unusually handsome and charming man and was often in the company of attractive women, he never wavered in his marriage vows.

When Ralph Bunche was at home, he enjoyed his family fully. Often the whole family attended sports events together. But Bunche was away so much that the family he loved suffered. They missed him as husband and as father.

In January 1946, Bunche was once more leaving home. He was appointed a member of the United Nations General Assembly and would attend the first session being held in London, England. Bunche sailed on the *Queen Mary*, along with Eleanor Roosevelt and other Americans. It was bitterly cold in England, and Bunche fell ill. He struggled to do his work, despite being diagnosed with diabetes, a common but serious disease in which the body cannot use sugar normally.

At the meetings, Bunche was frustrated by what he saw as a lack of professionalism in the American delegation. He thought his colleagues were "amateurs."[3]

After Norwegian diplomat Trygve Lie was appointed the first secretary-general of the United Nations in 1946, Bunche went to New York. At the time the United Nations headquarters were temporarily located at Hunter College in the Bronx. Bunche wanted to live in New York near his work, but his much-loved family home was in Washington, D.C. Bunche was working in New York and commuting home to Ruth and the children every weekend. It was not a good arrangement. Once again, Ruth Bunche ended up doing most of the parenting. Finally, the Bunches chose family togetherness over home ownership. They sold their house in Washington, D.C., and moved into an apartment in Parkway Village in New York City. The development was almost entirely occupied by United Nations employees. Now Bunche worked near home and could have a regular family life.

Bunche continued to do most of his work on the colonial problems the United Nations was trying to resolve. He ran the Trusteeship Council, which supervised the administration of territories placed under trusteeship—primarily former colonies, including those in Africa. Bunche was outstanding in his job. A colleague commented, "All that he did subsequently flowed from his knowledge, his experience, and his reputation as an expert on Africa."[4] In the early days of the United Nations, there was little firsthand knowledge of Africa from the viewpoint of black Africans. Bunche, from his research and travel, was able to provide valuable insights.

In 1947, an event took place that was to affect the course of history in the Middle East and to change

Ralph Bunche's life. Great Britain had ruled the area known as Palestine since 1917. But now Great Britain was turning its rule over to the United Nations. Palestine would soon be Ralph Bunche's problem.

Palestine has been home to Jews and Arabs for many centuries. Palestine has sacred places honored by Jews, Christians, and Muslims. About fifteen hundred years ago, Palestine was conquered by the Arabs. After World War I, Great Britain took over. Great Britain promised both the Jews and Arabs that they would have a homeland in Palestine. By the 1920s, there was rising tension between Jews and Arabs in Palestine. In the 1930s, many Jews fleeing Hitler's persecution had moved into the area, and the Arabs resented this new influx. Clashes between the two groups kept increasing.

After World War II ended, European Jews who had survived Hitler's persecution longed more than ever for a homeland where they could feel secure. The Arabs feared this would mean that they would be pushed out of homes they had occupied for centuries. The British could no longer deal with these conflicting interests, so they turned the rule of Palestine over to the United Nations.

The United Nations set up an eleven-member Special Committee on Palestine (UNSCOP). Bunche was appointed special assistant to the representative of the secretary-general of the United Nations. He and ten colleagues arrived in Palestine in June 1947. For the next six weeks, they covered two thousand miles gathering information. They interviewed Arabs and Jews, and the leaders of Egypt, Lebanon, Syria, TransJordan (now Jordan), and others. Bunche learned how difficult the Palestine problems were. Passions ran deep. Nobody wanted to talk about compromise, and for Bunche, the mental strain was very difficult.

Making matters worse, Bunche's eyes were irritated by the dust and heat of the region. Temperatures in Palestine soared, and winds blew the desert sand into Bunche's eyes. He was completely exhausted, his eyesight was failing, and he missed his family. Bunche was to have serious diabetes-related vision problems from this time on. Here, for the first time, he had to stop work entirely and rest his eyes. But finally Bunche and the others wrote a report, and UNSCOP adopted it as a blueprint for resolving the Palestine crisis. In late August 1947, Bunche headed home.

The UNSCOP report called for ending British rule in Palestine; preserving access to the holy places for all religions; and helping refugees who had lost their homes because of the unrest. Finally, the UNSCOP report called for the United Nations to rule Palestine until the transition to an Arab state, a Jewish state, and an international zone including Jerusalem.[5]

Bunche had been away from his family on his seventeenth wedding anniversary. Ruth Bunche had

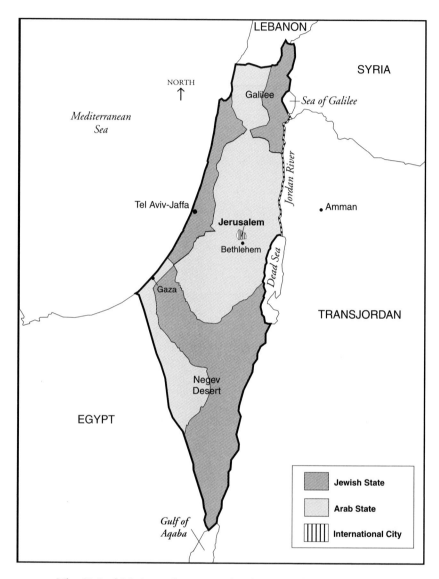

The United Nations plan: In 1947, the United Nations voted to divide the land known as Palestine (the area within the dark black line) into an Arab state and a Jewish state. The city of Jerusalem was to remain international. This plan never took effect.

Today, this region consists of the nation of Israel plus the Gaza Strip and the West Bank. Rule of the Gaza Strip and the West Bank, both largely populated by Arabs, has been in dispute for years, with both Arabs and Jews claiming the land.

spent the whole summer alone with the children. She was more than ready for normal family life to resume. From September 1947 to May 1948, the Bunches were together—they had eight months as a family before Bunche would once again take off for the dangers and hardships of Palestine.

The British withdrew from Palestine on schedule. Neither the Arab nor the Jewish residents were unhappy to see them go. But, unfortunately, Jews and Arabs now turned their wrath against each other. Arab terrorists attacked Jews. Jewish terrorists attacked Arabs. There were killings and counterkillings.

On May 14, 1948, the State of Israel was officially established. The Arab nations did not accept this, and they immediately attacked. A full-scale war broke out between Israel and its Arab neighbors. The United Nations quickly managed to arrange a cease-fire, but it was very shaky. Ralph Bunche received an urgent call from UN Secretary-General Trygve Lie. Bunche would have to arrive in Palestine in less than a week. He was to be chief representative of the secretary-general in Palestine. Bunche hurried to visit his daughters at their school in Pennsylvania. He packed his bags and once more said good-bye to Ruth Bunche and their son.

Bunche was on his way by May 23, 1948. He met Count Folke Bernadotte, the United Nations mediator for Palestine, for the first time on May 25. Despite their widely different backgrounds, Bunche and the

Ruth and Ralph Bunche with their five-year-old son, Ralph Jr.,
in 1948.

Swedish diplomat became good friends. When Count Bernadotte was assassinated just four months later, a grieving Ralph Bunche was left to lead the peace efforts in Palestine.

Ralph Bunche wrote a full report on the assassination of his friend and colleague Count Bernadotte. He knew the peace process would take a long time, so he cabled his wife to meet him in Paris. The Bunche daughters were still away at school, but Ruth Bunche and five-year-old Ralph Jr. boarded the *Queen Mary* in New York and sailed for Paris.

During October 1948, Ralph Bunche worked on the issue of security for United Nations officials in Palestine. For the first time in his career, he was his own boss. He answered only to the Security Council of the United Nations. He was on the scene, and he was the expert. When the General Assembly of the United Nations met in Paris, Bunche pointed out that UN personnel were unarmed. "Their only protection is the United Nations armband and the United Nations flag, often accompanied by a white flag," he said.[6] Bunche pleaded for the Arabs and Jews to respect the safety of the brave peacekeepers.

In October 1948, an Egyptian attack on an Israeli convoy was followed by an all-out Jewish attack on Arab-populated Galilee. The fragile truce had broken down completely. Bunche hurried between Tel Aviv and Cairo through the fall and the winter of 1948, trying to stop the violence. The fierce fighting continued while Bunche battled many petty jealousies among the United Nations officials. United Nations Secretary-General Lie yelled at Bunche across a lunch table in Paris, "You are good number 2 man, but not a number 1."[7] But Bunche worked on with superhuman effort. On January 6, 1949, Bunche announced he had achieved a cease-fire. At last the guns fell silent. At the war's end, the Arab-Israeli borders did not follow the United Nations plan of 1947. Instead, Israel was larger, Egypt held the Gaza Strip, and Jordon held the West Bank.

7

NOBEL
LAUREATE

istorian J. C. Hurewitz described Ralph Bunche as having "a highly attuned sense of challenge and opportunity."[1] Hurewitz called Bunche "by far the best informed international expert on the Palestine problem."[2] Bunche needed all the skills at his command when the Egyptian and Israeli delegations arrived at the Hotel del Roses in Rhodes. They had come to talk peace but were very hostile. The members of the delegations went so far as to avoid looking at one another in the hotel lobby. When their paths crossed, they turned their backs to one another.

Since the Israelis and the Egyptians would not even

meet face-to-face, Bunche met separately with each delegation in his hotel suite. With persistent charm, he had finally persuaded both delegations to meet there. Israeli delegate Shabtai Rosenne recalled, "My most vivid recollection of this physically huge man—handsome and attractive," was his "bubbling sense of humor."[3] Bunche presided over the first gatherings from a sofa while the Israeli and Egyptian delegations sat in silence. They addressed all their comments to Bunche, refusing to talk directly to one another. Rosenne remembered that Bunche was tough. "He could be harsh, he cajoled, he threatened, and he charmed."[4] Once an enraged Israeli delegate tossed a pencil in the air to make a point. The pencil bounced and hit an Arab delegate. This minor incident almost ended the peace talks then and there. Bunche somehow got the Israeli delegate to apologize to the Arab delegate in vague terms, and that saved the peace process.

After six weeks of talks at the hotel, the mood changed dramatically. The Egyptians and Israelis gradually exchanged a few words indirectly, and then they were arguing person-to-person. There were even moments of genuine friendliness. When an Egyptian negotiator became ill, some Israelis went to his bedside to offer good wishes.

Bunche worked relentlessly to iron out the final wording in the armistice agreement that arose from the talks. The agreement was signed February 23, 1949, in the hotel beneath a mural of Adam and Eve leaving the Garden of Eden. Bunche threw a party to celebrate. The Egyptians sent in a special plane load of delicacies. An Israeli delegate later recalled the festive scene. "I well remember sitting with the head of the Egyptian delegation as he showed me photographs of his family. It was an atmosphere as different as one could imagine from that of the first day in the corridor with its averted heads."[5]

Before the final agreement was reached, Bunche had purchased some pottery plates and had each inscribed

Bunche, as United Nations Acting Mediator, signs the peace treaty between the Egyptian and Israeli governments. At right is Bunche's political advisor, Henri Vigier.

"Rhodes Armistice Talks—1949." His plan was to give the Israeli and Egyptian delegates the plates as mementos of the grand occasion. On the day that he gave out the pottery, he told everyone he would have broken the plates over their heads if they had refused to compromise.[6]

Congratulations flooded in from all over the world. Ruth Bunche, despite the months of painful loneliness, said she was "proud and happy" for her husband.[7] President Harry Truman praised Bunche's work and the great contribution he had made to peace in the Middle East.

A peace agreement between Israel and Jordan was concluded in April 1949. Bunche went to Paris to relax. He was worn out physically and mentally. But when he appeared for dinner at restaurants in France, his presence was hailed with music and cheers. Ralph Bunche had become a world hero. He had picked up the peace process from his assassinated predecessor— Count Bernadotte—and produced a near-miracle with his hard work.

Bunche decided he would continue the Middle East peace process from New York. He would supervise the peace talks between Israel and Syria from there. Bunche arrived in New York on April 18, 1949, to a hero's welcome. Israeli leader Ben-Gurion said of him, "Dr. Bunche handled the negotiations with great skill and gradually brought the two sides closer to agreement, initially on minor questions, and then on major ones as well."[8]

Another Israeli leader, Moshe Dayan, said of Bunche, "He spoke little and listened to others with intense concentration"; he "displayed a great deal of charm"; and he "created a mood of amiability and trust."[9] Fellow negotiator Pablo de Azcarate of Spain praised Bunche as a man of "great intelligence and exceptional energy."[10]

In August 1949, the official mediator post for Palestine was abolished. The United Nations expressed its deep thanks to Bunche for his wonderful devotion to duty.

Upon his return to the United States, Bunche was offered many college jobs, including positions at prestigious schools like Harvard, Stanford, the University of California at Berkeley, and the University of Pennsylvania. He received awards and honors at numerous testimonial dinners. At one such dinner, Bunche expressed his deep loathing of war. "I have a number of very strong biases," Bunche said, listing them as being against "hate and intolerance, racial and religious bigotry and war."[11] Bunche saw hatred among peoples as leading to division and war.

On April 21, 1949, Bunche was offered a job as assistant secretary of state for Near Eastern, South Asian, and African affairs. In May he visited President Truman to turn down the job. Bunche simply did not want to bring his family back to Washington and its atmosphere of prejudice. Years earlier when the Bunche family dog had died and the family went to the local pet cemetery, they were told that pets of African Americans had to be buried separately from the pets of white owners. It was a small but painful example of the day-to-day racial insults an African-American family had to endure. Also, Bunche had decided to continue working for the United Nations.

In July 1949, Bunche was awarded the Spingarn Medal at the fortieth Annual Convention of the National Association for the Advancement of Colored People (NAACP). The gold medal is given each year for the highest or noblest achievement by an African American.

In the summer of 1949, an agreement was finally signed between Syria and Israel. Bunche was finally free of the Palestine problem that had consumed his energies for more than two years. In July, the Bunches enjoyed a rare holiday in Los Angeles at the home of Will Rogers, Jr., son of the popular American cowboy humorist, actor, and aviator.

In September 1950, Bunche was told he was being awarded the Nobel Peace Prize. His first reaction was that he should not even accept the prize. He had worked so hard in Palestine because he believed in peace. He did not do it so he could win a prize.[12] President Truman called to congratulate Bunche, and

United Nations Secretary-General Trygve Lie urged Bunche to accept the prize because it would be good publicity for the organization's peace efforts.

On his European journey to accept the Nobel Peace Prize, Bunche stopped off in Rome for a visit with Pope Pius XII. Then, on December 10, Ruth and Ralph Bunche arrived in Oslo, Norway. Bunche gave the Nobel lecture in the Aula (great hall) of Oslo University. He said, "If today we speak of peace, we also speak of the United Nations, for in this era, peace and the United Nations have become inseparable. If the United Nations cannot ensure peace, there will be none."[13] Bunche also said, "Who . . . could be so unseeing as not to realize that in modern war, victory is illusory; that the harvest of war can be only misery, destruction and degradation?"[14]

Ralph Bunche was the first person of African ancestry to win the Nobel Peace Prize. The central themes of his speeches and writings in the 1950s were the value of the United Nations to humanity and the need to achieve racial equality. He talked to organizations and colleges. He gave as many as five speeches a month and was awarded twelve honorary degrees in the early 1950s. Bunche saw early on that racial equality and world harmony depended on every person's having a decent standard of living. He wrote, "The titanic conflicts of the future will be between those who have and those who have not."[15]

Joan and Ralph Jr. congratulate their father for winning the Nobel Peace Prize.

Bunche returned to work in the Trusteeship Department of the United Nations in 1951. He was now able to spend most of his time in the United States. Family life flourished for the Bunches. Then a sudden illness struck seven-year-old Ralph Jr. The boy fell ill with a fever and stiff neck. He was found to be suffering from polio—a dread disease that paralyzed and killed thousands, often children. The Bunches kept a long and anxious vigil, rarely leaving their son's bedside. Many children who recovered from polio could no longer breathe or walk normally. Some spent their lives breathing with the aid of a gigantic "iron lung." Others walked with braces on their legs or with crutches. Polio was one of the most feared diseases of the time. Fortunately, Ralph Jr. recovered completely and suffered no serious disability.

Weary of apartment living, the Bunches moved to a new home on Grosvenor Road in Kew Gardens, Queens, New York. The large house had a nice garden and it was ideal for the family's needs.

During the early 1950s, the Korean War raged. Ralph Bunche saw that war as a vital test of the ability of the United Nations to stop the aggression of one nation against another. The Korean War had begun in June 1950 when Communist North Korea invaded South Korea. The United Nations voted to send in troops to protect South Korea. The troops—the majority of whom were American—were led by the United

After he won the Nobel Peace Prize, Ralph Bunche often gave as many as five speeches a month for audiences around the nation.

States. These forces reversed the North Korean attack and then invaded North Korea itself; as a result China entered the war on the side of North Korea. An armistice was finally signed in 1953 on the basis of the original border between the two Koreas.

In March 1951, Bunche was invited to speak at a University of Virginia legal forum. The student who invited Bunche was Robert F. Kennedy (future United States senator and brother of President John F. Kennedy). Bunche wrote to Robert Kennedy that he would be glad to speak, but his audience would have to be desegregated. This college town in Charlottesville, Virginia, was still unwilling to see black and white people seated together in any gathering. "As a matter of firm principle," Bunche wrote, "I never appear before a segregated audience."[16] Young Robert Kennedy had a major struggle with some of the students, but in the end he provided an integrated audience and Bunche spoke.

Also in 1951, Bunche was the commencement speaker at Morgan State College in Baltimore, Maryland. "The practices and incidents of racial bigotry can only be intolerably offensive to every fair-minded and right thinking American," he said.[17] However, Bunche warned the African-American students never to use their race as an excuse for not even trying—for that failure could not be blamed on bigotry.

"The cry of discrimination must never be used as an alibi for lack of effort, preparation, and ability," he said.[18]

Bunche's United Nations work in the early 1950s was fairly routine, and his family enjoyed a rest from his usually hectic schedule. The Bunches attended plays, musicals, and the opera. They had an active social life. Bunche was an enthusiastic baseball fan, and he became good friends with Jackie Robinson, an outstanding player on the Brooklyn Dodgers team. Robinson became the first black major-league baseball player in 1947. Prior to this, all the major-league players were white, and black players had to play in their own league.

Like Jackie Robinson, Ralph Bunche was an inspiration to young African Americans. Prominent African-American historian John Hope Franklin said, "Negroes were heartened when Ralph Bunche joined the United Nations" because they hoped he might "advance substantially the welfare and interests of those people who would be unable to promote their own interests."[19]

In the 1950s, there was deep hostility between the non-Communist world led by the United States, and the Communist world led by the Soviet Union. This hostility was known as the Cold War. Many Americans feared that the Communists would take over the United States. In 1945, at the end of World War II, the Soviet

Union had extended its power over Eastern Europe. In 1949, China became Communist, too.

All over the world it seemed that Communism was on the march. Some Communist spies were discovered in the United States. There was growing fear that Communist spies were all over the place. Some of the fear turned into hysteria, a form of "witch-hunting," with people seeing Communist influence everywhere. The lives of prominent Americans were searched for evidence of Communist sympathies. The dark shadows of this fear fell upon the life and career of Ralph Bunche.

8

CONGO CRISIS

he United States Senate Internal Security Subcommittee was very distrustful of the United Nations. In the climate of fear that spread through the United States at the time, some were afraid that Communist spies might be entering the country under the guise of United Nations diplomats. People who worked for the United Nations were eyed with suspicion. American employees of the United Nations were fingerprinted by the Federal Bureau of Investigation (FBI) to make it easier to check their backgrounds. Ralph Bunche was investigated, too.

In March 1953, Ralph Bunche was called before

the Senate subcommittee. The senators knew that Bunche had been part of the National Negro Congress (NNC), which later became a pro-Communist organization. The senators questioned Bunche about the NNC. Bunche was asked whether he had ever been a member of the Communist Party. Bunche had not, and he told the senators this.

When it became publicly known that Bunche was

In 1953, when the fear of communism was sweeping the nation, Bunche remained devoted to his country and joined his old friend Eleanor Roosevelt at a memorial service for former president Franklin D. Roosevelt.

under investigation, some members of the press began to attack Bunche and call the United Nations a tool of communism. Bunche could not believe his loyalty could be questioned after all his years of public service. He was deeply hurt that anyone doubted his devotion to his country.[1]

During this stressful time in Bunche's life, he was also besieged by family problems. Ruth Bunche was in poor health. Daughter Jane, a student at Radcliffe College, was suffering from severe depression and undergoing psychiatric treatment. Bunche struggled to cope with all this while having to prove his loyalty to Senate investigators.

Ralph Bunche's life was examined with a fine-tooth comb. He spent days having to dig through old files and opening boxes and trunks that had been closed for years. Bunche needed to find copies of letters he had sent years before. It was painful and humiliating. Bunche had to refute so many detailed accusations that he ended up writing more than one hundred pages explaining long-forgotten details of his life from his student days to the present.

Because Ralph Bunche was always concerned with the economic and political rights of African Americans, he often belonged to groups fighting for these goals. Communists seeking to gain the support of African-American students and educators often joined these groups, too. Membership in a group infiltrated by Communists was seen as questionable.[2] But Communist dogma, or beliefs, had never attracted Bunche.[3] Whenever he belonged to a group working for civil rights and it became pro-Communist, he left immediately.

On May 28, 1954, the Senate subcommittee came to the conclusion that there was no credible basis for any of the accusations leveled against Bunche, and the sad episode was officially closed. However, from time to time, attacks on Bunche's character recurred, based largely on the fact that he worked for the United Nations, which was mistrusted by some people.

In August 1954, the new secretary-general of the United Nations, Dag Hammarskjöld, chose Bunche to be one of the undersecretaries for special political affairs. Bunche began his new job in January 1955. At the same time, he became a trustee of the Rockefeller Foundation. This foundation was created in 1917 by John D. Rockefeller to promote the well-being of humanity. It supported research in medicine and science, farming, and the political and social sciences.

Bunche became one of Hammarskjöld's most trusted United Nations colleagues as they worked together on several world problems. Bunche had no fixed assignment, but his first task was to promote peaceful uses for atomic energy. In 1955, Bunche also spent time in Latin America and in Europe on United Nations business. He was in constant pain with kidney trouble and a slipped disk in his back.

In September 1956, Jane Bunche married Burton Pierce, a young administrator at Harvard Business School. As the Bunche family was celebrating this happy occasion, a serious new crisis flared up in the Middle East. Israelis raided the Gaza Strip, and Palestinian Arabs attacked Israeli targets. Egyptian President Gamal Abdel Nasser nationalized the Suez Canal, which had been controlled by the French and British since 1875.

Israel, France, and Great Britain demanded that Egypt withdraw its forces ten miles from the Suez Canal. When Egypt refused, the three nations used military force. With the support of the United States, the United Nations demanded an end to the attack on Egypt. Bunche drafted cables to Great Britain, France, and Israel, and President Eisenhower threw his total support behind a United Nations–brokered settlement of the crisis. A cease-fire took effect in November 1956.

A United Nations Emergency Force was set up to keep the peace around the Suez Canal. On November 15, 1956, United Nations troops arrived in Egypt. Bunche considered this a great achievement. "For the first time we have found a way to use military men for peace instead of war," he said.[4] Bunche conducted

In October 1956, Ralph Bunche met with President Dwight D. Eisenhower to discuss the crisis over the Suez Canal in the Middle East.

meetings with the leaders in the area over the next several months, and gradually the crisis was resolved. The Suez Canal, closed during part of the crisis, was reopened in 1957 under Egyptian control. Full-scale war had been averted.

Bunche returned home to New York in April 1957. He wrote a letter to President Eisenhower about civil rights. The Civil Rights Bill of 1957 was under consideration, and Bunche urged the president not to allow it to be weakened.[5]

The Bunches welcomed their first grandchild, Karen Pierce, on July 8, 1957, but Bunche could not remain at home long to enjoy the grandchild. Though he was again suffering poor health, he had to return to the Middle East for more conferences related to problems in Lebanon. Bunche's health had been seriously deteriorating since the mid-1950s. His diabetes was taking a terrible toll on him. Between January and June of 1958, Bunche lost thirty-five pounds.

Bunche's illness was made worse by a decision he had made. To control his diabetes, Bunche had to give himself shots of insulin. He felt that he was "enslaved" by insulin, so he simply stopped injecting himself.[6] The consequences were drastic, and Bunche almost died. He resumed his regimen of insulin, and his health had improved by November 1958. Still, he was drained and weary as he traveled to the Middle East to work on the Lebanon crisis.

Lebanon, an Arab state with Islamic and Christian people, was friendly to the United States. Suddenly there was a revolution, started by a group of strong Arab nationalists who were hostile to the United States. United States marines were sent to put down the revolution in Lebanon. Eventually, the crisis eased and a healthier Ralph Bunche visited Egypt, Israel, Jordan, and Palestinian areas to help quell any new flare-ups of tension there. The Middle East seemed to be at least temporarily more peaceful, but another nightmarish crisis was about to erupt, this time in Africa. Once again all of Bunche's powers of persuasion and courage would be called into use.

In 1957, Ralph Bunche had taken part in a happy African occasion: the people of Ghana celebrating their independence. Bunche had visited many African countries on the verge of independence. But now it was 1960, and in the Belgian Congo an explosion of violence was brewing.

The Congo had been brutally ruled by the Belgians since 1885. King Leopold II of Belgium allowed private companies to develop the rich mining areas of the Congo. African workers were treated with extreme cruelty. In 1960, when the Congo became independent, Bunche was on hand as the UN representative. Patrice Lumumba was elected as Congo's first president.

Immediately after Lumumba was installed as president, other political factions fought for power.

Violence allegedly promoted by factions wanting to restore Belgian rule broke out. The situation quickly turned to chaos. Europeans living in the country were fleeing for their lives.

As the United Nations representative, Ralph Bunche tried to work with Congo's President Lumumba, but Bunche's efforts to establish a working relationship with Lumumba turned out to be a disaster. Bunche was deeply upset by Lumumba's mood swings and unreasonable behavior.

President Lumumba was kidnapped and later killed by rivals, and the capital, Leopoldville, became unsafe, especially for foreigners. Bunche later described one dangerous incident of this period. "We were all frightened silly in Leopoldville that day," he wrote. "I was particularly frightened because I scare easily anyway." Bunche described looking out of his hotel room window: "I saw that those Congolese soldiers had already imbibed too much beer, obviously that scared me even more."[7]

As Bunche stood in the doorway of his room, one of the soldiers pointed a rifle at his head. Bunche ducked back inside just as the rifle fired, and he just barely escaped injury. Then three of the soldiers burst into the room. Because of Bunche's light skin color, they thought he was a Belgian. Feelings ran high against Belgians because of the abuses during the long colonial rule. The soldiers began to arrest Bunche. "I just took it for granted I was a 'goner,'" that they were going to "take me out and stand me against a wall and shoot me."[8] Fortunately, the soldiers merely ordered Bunche and his aides downstairs into the lobby and then left.

As law and order collapsed in the Congo, the United Nations Security Council held an emergency meeting. The United Nations assembled the French-named Organization des Nations Unies au Congo (ONUC) with soldiers mainly from other African nations. Hammarskjöld put Bunche in charge of the whole operation. He worked from his hotel room with two assistants and one secretary.

Ralph Bunche personally supervised the deployment of thousands of United Nations troops who filled in as the Belgian troops withdrew. He steadily increased the number of UN troops to handle lawlessness in the streets. It was a huge job. Wearing a fatigue cap like an officer directing a major battle operation in wartime, Bunche was on the job almost twenty-four hours a day during the initial deployment. He got the troops to their proper places, supplied them, and gave them their orders.

In August 1960, two of Bunche's security men were arrested and threatened with death. They were rescued just in the nick of time. The incident added to Bunche's stress. He lost his appetite and a varicose ulcer on his leg was giving him serious trouble.

After spending nearly two months in the dangerous chaos of the Congo, Bunche returned to the United States. The conflict in the Congo raged on. It would cost Bunche many more harrowing days before it was finally resolved. It would also cost him the life of another very dear friend.

9

YEMEN, CYPRUS, VIETNAM

n January 1961, the United Nations tried to help the new leader of the Congo—Joseph Kasavubu—keep order. The UN formed a group of senior officials called "the Congo Club" to assist Kasavubu. Ralph Bunche was a member of this club, and he spent long hours attempting to resolve the crisis.

In June 1961, Bunche was fifty-eight years old. He wanted to spend more time with his family. He also wanted to have time to promote civil rights issues in the United States.[1] So he submitted his resignation to the United Nations. But Secretary-General Hammarskjöld persuaded Bunche to remain on the job. Their friendship and Bunche's respect for Hammarskjöld were great enough to be the deciding factors.

In September 1961, Hammarskjöld himself flew to the Congo to try to mediate the dispute now tearing the country apart. Moise Tshombe was leading a revolt in mineral-rich Katanga province, which was trying to secede from the new Congo. Hammarskjöld was on his way to meet Tshombe in northern Rhodesia when his plane was reported missing. On September 18, Ralph Bunche was given the tragic news. Wreckage from the plane was sighted. There were no survivors. For Bunche it was a painful loss of a cherished friend and a fellow fighter for peace. On September 22, Bunche nominated Hammarskjöld for the Nobel Peace Prize. In November, it was awarded to the fallen UN secretary-general.

Burma's U Thant was appointed the next secretary-general of the United Nations. Like Hammarskjöld, U Thant was courageous. He had already heard much about Ralph Bunche, and he wanted him for his right-hand man.[2] U Thant described Bunche as "the most effective and best known of international civil servants."[3] Bunche promised to remain at the United Nations during U Thant's term, which began in November 1961.

For two and a half years, Bunche was involved in the Congo crisis. By April 1963, the crisis had subsided

Ralph Bunche holds a meeting aboard an aircraft in the Belgian Congo in 1961. All of Bunche's diplomatic powers of persuasion and courage were called on to settle this raging conflict in Africa.

and some order returned to the country. Bunche now had time for other activities.

In June 1963, Bunche returned to the United States to attend the funeral of Medgar Evers, a civil rights activist who had been murdered. Bunche called Evers a "dedicated and courageous man, who died for a cause as righteous as any cause can be, and who was a hero and is a martyr in the truest and noblest sense. . . ."[4]

In 1963, another Middle East crisis occurred. The Republic of Yemen, a small country on the south coast

Ralph Bunche speaks with Charles Evers (brother of slain civil rights activist Medgar Evers) and Myrlie Evers (widow of Medgar Evers). At the right is A. D. Bertel, president of Tougaloo College in Mississippi.

of the Arabian peninsula, became independent in 1918 after long years of Turkish rule. Now fighting had broken out between two groups. One group was loyal to the king of Yemen and friendly with Saudi Arabia. The other group was allied with Egypt.

As head of the United Nations Yemen Observor Mission, Bunche was sent to Yemen on orders of Secretary-General U Thant. When Bunche arrived in Taiz, his car was immediately surrounded by an unruly crowd burning effigies—crude figures representing their enemies. The air was thick with smoke. The crowd rocked the car back and forth so violently that Bunche feared his last hour may well have come.[5]

The car was an old but sturdy one, and it was over-heating, threatening to spray the already furious crowd with boiling hot steam and water from its radiator. Such an occurrence would have brought down the murderous wrath of the scalded demonstrators.

Bunche's driver skillfully inched the car forward. He managed to get free of the crowd and turned off the main road. Racing furiously across a field with the screaming crowd in pursuit, he managed an escape down a side street.

When Bunche got back to his hotel, he found cake, chocolates, oranges, and whiskey waiting for him. These gifts were from Egypt, which hoped to win Bunche over to its side in the dispute.

Bunche began to work intensively to get a fair

agreement. He flew to a desert outpost to meet tribal chieftains for their input. Stepping from the plane, he was greeted by rifle-toting chieftains who formed a circle around him. The elder of the group started reading something Bunche did not understand. A sudden uproar began. The armed men waved their rifles and glittering curved knives. "I got scared," Bunche later recalled.[6] But he soon learned the excited men were not angry at him. The emotional show was staged to persuade Bunche to lead them in battle against the enemy. They saw the handsome American as an ideal warrior for their cause. An Egyptian officer standing nearby presented Bunche with candy wrapped in bright tinfoil, and everybody settled down to talk.[7]

Bunche finally reached an agreement in Yemen. In the agreement, Yemen remained independent. The United Nations would send a force to maintain the peace. Although more trouble arose in Yemen later on, the immediate crisis had been resolved, and Bunche headed home again. In the summer of 1963 Bunche took his wife and son on a European vacation.

On August 28, 1963, when Dr. Martin Luther King, Jr., led a large civil rights march on Washington, D.C., Ralph Bunche participated. That September, Bunche escorted U Thant to a meeting with President John F. Kennedy at the White House. Two months later Ralph Bunche and U Thant walked together in the funeral procession for the assassinated president.

In October 1963, President Kennedy had chosen Ralph Bunche to receive the Presidential Medal of Freedom. The medal is given to honor American civilians who have made outstanding contributions to national security and world peace. Bunche received the medal on December 6, 1963, expressing his personal sadness that he could not be happy on the occasion because of the tragic loss of President Kennedy.[8]

There were occasions in 1964 when Ruth and Ralph Bunche could take time for some recreation. They both enjoyed attending Metropolitan Opera performances. But there was always the next crisis lurking on the horizon. Just when the Bunches settled down to normal family life, an ominous phone call yanked Ralph Bunche back to a world hot spot. In early 1964 the crisis was in Cyprus.

Cyprus is an island in the eastern Mediterranean Sea off the Turkish coast. The majority of the people in Cyprus were of Greek ancestry, and the minority were Turks. In 1959, an agreement gave equal rights to both groups, but unrest turned into open fighting. By 1964, Greeks and Turks were battling each other. The United Nations set up the United Nations Force in Cyprus, and Ralph Bunche oversaw the operation. Temporary peace was secured, but the Cyprus crisis has continued to boil over in the decades since.

In 1964, Ralph Bunche's poor health was becoming

Dr. Bunche visited Tougaloo College in Mississippi to help celebrate United Nations Day.

more and more of a problem. Failing eyesight hampered his work. The dust and heat of places like Cyprus, Yemen, and other Middle East countries aggravated the problem. Bunche relied on notes in large print and struggled on. No sooner had the crisis in Cyprus cooled down than a bitter, bloody conflict erupted in Kashmir. Soon Ralph Bunche was flying over the Himalayas and bouncing along in jeeps over dirt roads in India and Pakistan.

Kashmir is a mostly Muslim region in northwest India. It was claimed by both India and Pakistan. India and Pakistan began fighting over Kashmir in 1947. A United Nations force—United Nations Military Observer Group—had been there since 1948. Now armed groups from both sides were in full-scale battle. Bunche took charge of the worsening crisis and asked the UN Security Council to order a cease-fire at once. India and Pakistan agreed to the cease-fire, and another dangerous world crisis was defused with the help of Ralph Bunche.

When the Bunches took a brief respite from his United Nations work in July 1966 to visit Monaco, near-tragedy resulted. The Bunches had been invited to Monaco by Prince Rainier and his wife, Princess Grace (the former actress Grace Kelly), who was a friend of the Bunches. Ralph Bunche tripped on a step and bruised his toe. An infection resulted. Such infections are extremely dangerous for diabetics and can result in

Prime Minister Jawaharal Nehru of India, left, spoke with Ralph Bunche in the United States in 1949.

the need to amputate limbs. When Bunche returned to New York, the infection was so severe he was immediately hospitalized. During a month-long stay in the hospital, doctors told Bunche he had come very close to losing his leg.

In the mid-1960s, Ralph Bunche was troubled by an issue that would later divide most of America—the war in Vietnam. Since 1964, American involvement in the war between Communists in Vietnam and non-Communists was increasing. The United States was fighting on the side of South Vietnam to prevent a Communist victory. United States sent more and more troops. Casualties mounted on both sides. This war was to strike the Bunches in a very personal way.

10

DEATH OF A PEACEMAKER

R alph Bunche strongly opposed United States involvement in the Vietnam War. He did not want to state his views publicly because this would reduce his effectiveness at the United Nations. Instead, Bunche worked with UN Secretary-General U Thant to try to find a diplomatic solution to end the Vietnam War.[1]

U Thant was deeply troubled by the deaths of civilians in Vietnam. "One does not have to be a pacifist to condemn the napalming and dropping of anti-personnel bombs on hamlets from 35,000 feet above," U Thant said.[2] He hoped Bunche could talk to President

Lyndon Johnson about ending the war. Bunche and U Thant visited President Johnson in August 1964. They urged him to conduct immediate negotiations to end the war.[3]

When he was United States ambassador to the United Nations, Adlai Stevenson was sympathetic to Bunche's peace efforts, but Stevenson died in July 1965. Later efforts by U Thant and Bunche to broker peace talks between the United States and North Vietnam were unsuccessful. The Vietnam War raged on, described by Ralph Bunche as a war "no one can win, which makes it senseless and incomprehensible."[4]

A terrible tragedy struck the Bunche family on October 9, 1966. Jane Pierce, the younger Bunche daughter, committed suicide by jumping off the roof of her twelve-story apartment building. The thirty-four-year-old woman had suffered from psychiatric problems for a long time. The heartbreaking loss of their daughter plunged the Bunches into deep sorrow. Ralph Bunche was despondent for two years. He kept thinking about his daughter's life and how things might have been different. Jane had married young, and though she was brilliant, she was often depressed. Bunche worried that his own long absences from home had contributed to his daughter's deep sadness. He tortured himself with guilt that he had not shown her enough love and attention.[5]

As Bunche grieved for his daughter, Ralph Bunche,

Ralph Bunche and United Nations Secretary-General U Thant meet with President Lyndon Johnson to discuss an end to the Vietnam War.

Jr., reported for military service in the Vietnam War. Bunche had lost his beloved daughter. Now his son was about to join in the fighting of a war that Bunche completely opposed.[6] Ralph Bunche, Jr., went to war anyway, and two years later he returned safely.

During this sad period of Bunche's life, his health declined dramatically. Many ailments caused by his diabetes worsened. Bunche could no longer read the notes in block letters that he had written on large-print typewriters. Bunche suffered frequently from weakness and fatigue. In 1967, he lost his driver's license because of the progressive deterioration of his eyesight. Bunche now had to rely entirely on United Nations security men to get him where he needed to go.

Bunche was losing feeling in his toes, and he had a pinched nerve in his neck. Bursitis, a painful inflammation, plagued him in his right hip. Because of all this, retirement seemed the only sensible decision. Bunche sent a formal letter of resignation to the United Nations. But once again he changed his mind. U Thant pleaded with Bunche to remain and he did. It was a fateful decision. He had promised his wife that now, at last, they would have time for peaceful family vacations and a normal life. Bunche did not know it then, but by refusing to retire, he was ending any hopes the Bunches had for enjoying their retirement years together.

In 1967, there was yet another world crisis, and

the ailing Bunche would suffer a crushing blow to his confidence in Middle East peace. Bunche had worked long and hard to resolve the conflicts between Israel and its Arab neighbors. Now what was called the Six-Day War broke out on June 5, 1967. Egyptian troops closed a convenient Israeli water route to east Africa and Asia, and soon war raged between Israel and the Arab countries of Egypt, Jordan, Syria, and others.

The Israelis won, gaining more territory, and the United Nations arranged a cease-fire on June 10, 1967. But it was obvious that real peace was not restored and that there would be future wars and more violence. The triumph of Ralph Bunche at Rhodes that glorious day in January 1949 had been tarnished by bloody new realities.

Ralph Bunche missed the twentieth anniversary celebration of the founding of the United Nations in San Francisco. He was not well enough to attend. In December 1968, president-elect Richard Nixon visited Bunche and U Thant to thank them for their efforts toward world peace. In May 1969, Bunche attended the dedication of Ralph Bunche Hall at the University of California at Los Angeles, his alma mater. The eleven-story structure was the tallest building on the UCLA campus. It served as the home of the social science departments. Bunche gave a stirring speech on the occasion, citing his love for peace.

In July and August 1969, Ruth and Ralph Bunche

President Richard M. Nixon with Ralph Bunche, far right, and U Thant, center, secretary-general of the United Nations.

took their last vacation together. They visited Honolulu, Tokyo, Manila, Hong Kong, Bangkok, New Delhi, Teheran, Istanbul, and Beirut. Ralph Bunche enjoyed the trip, but he had an attack of retinal bleeding in one of his eyes. He also suffered from arthritis, bursitis, nausea, sinus trouble, and loss of feeling in his fingers and toes. It was obvious that he could not look forward to a long life, yet he made the most of each day. And he had not yet given up his job at the United Nations.

Though now mortally ill and nearly blind, Bunche negotiated in 1969 with the shah of Iran to resolve a crisis in Bahrain, a small Persian Gulf state. British negotiator Anthony Parsons marveled at how Bunche, despite his terrible physical condition, was totally devoted to solving this latest crisis.[7] With an agreement on Bahrain secured, Bunche flew to Geneva to seal the deal. U Thant warmly praised Bunche's efforts in Bahrain as turning the tide for peace.

In August 1970, Bunche fell and broke a rib. Fits of hiccups delayed his healing. Bunche was now unable to see faces clearly, but his brilliant mind remained sharp. To help cope with blindness, Bunche relied on something he had always loved—music. It became even more important to him now.

In early 1971, Bunche was often absent from his office. His last official act was attending a United Nations meeting on May 17, 1971. In June, he broke his right arm. He fell into a coma for several days, while his wife, son, and daughter Joan remained at his bedside. At the time, Joan Bunche worked at the UN Secretariat on Economic Development. In July, Bunche rallied from the coma and underwent dialysis to treat his kidney failure. He was formally relieved of his duties at the United Nations.

Bunche was in and out of New York Hospital in the summer and fall of 1971. He died peacefully there at 12:40 A.M. on December 9, 1971. The United Nations General Assembly stood for a moment of silence in tribute. The funeral was held on December 11 at Riverside Church in New York. At the service, famed African-American opera singer Leontyne Price sang "I Want Jesus to Walk with Me." Bunche was buried at Woodlawn Cemetery in the Bronx in the Bunche family plot.

U Thant said of his fallen friend Ralph Bunche that he was "an international institution" who transcended "both nationality and race."[8] In its January 1, 1972, issue, the *New Yorker* magazine called Bunche "one of the greatest Americans of our clouded, mind-numbing times."[9] Vernon Jordan of the Urban League said Bunche had been an "inspirational beacon to young black people."[10] Roy Wilkins of the NAACP paid tribute to Bunche's devotion to making sure African Americans were treated with equality in their own land.[11]

He was eulogized as "kindness itself."[12] Coworkers

Ralph Bunche, the first African American to win the Nobel Peace Prize, devoted his life to his vision of a better world.

One of Ralph Bunche's favorite quotes from the Bible is inscribed on the wall of Ralph Bunche Park in New York City.

recalled that no matter how great the crisis they worked on, Bunche would take time to ask "how the children were," including his entire staff in his warm concern.[13]

In 1980, a large steel sculpture dedicated to Ralph Bunche was created by African-American artist Daniel Johnson. Johnson's father knew Bunche as a youth in Los Angles. The monolithic sculpture, dedicated to peace, stands in a small park on First Avenue in New York City, facing the entrance to the United Nations. The park is called Ralph Bunche Park. It offers a fitting tribute to a quiet, humble man who literally gave his life to the noblest battle of all—the struggle against violence, hatred, and war.

CHRONOLOGY

1904—Born in Detroit, Michigan, on August 7.

1918—Graduates from Thirtieth Street Intermediate School in Los Angeles, California.

1922—Valedictorian at graduation from Jefferson High School in Los Angeles.

1927—Graduates summa cum laude from the University of California at Los Angeles.

1928—Master of arts degree in political science awarded by Harvard University; organizes and chairs first Political Science Department, Howard University, Washington, D.C.

1930—Marries Ruth Ethel Harris in June.

1931—First child, Joan, born in December; awarded Julius Rosenwald Fellowship for African research.

1933—Second child, Jane, born in May.

1934—Completes Ph.D. in political science and international relations at Harvard University.

1939—Participates in Carnegie study by Swedish sociologist Gunnar Myrdal, leading to publication of major study on race relations in the United States.

1943—Third child, Ralph Jr., born in September.

1944—Joins State Department.

1945—Advisor to United States delegation at San Francisco conference drafting UN Charter.

1946—Member United States delegation at first session of UN General Assembly in London.

1948—Appointed representative of secretary-general with United Nations mediator in Palestine, Count Bernadotte; succeeds the assassinated Bernadotte as acting mediator in September.

1949—Successfully negotiates armistice between Israel and Egypt; awarded the Spingarn Medal by the NAACP.

1950—Awarded Nobel Peace Prize.

1955—Assumes position as an undersecretary of the United Nations; becomes trustee of Rockefeller Foundation.

1956—Organizes and directs UN peacekeeping during Suez crisis.

1963—Receives Presidential Medal of Freedom.

1971—Retires from the United Nations; dies on December 9.

CHAPTER NOTES

Chapter 1. Assassination in Jerusalem

1. Brian Urquhart, *Ralph Bunche: An American Life* (New York: W. W. Norton & Company, 1993), p. 168.

2. Benjamin Rivlin, "The Legacy of Ralph Bunche," in *Ralph Bunche: The Man and His Times*, ed. Benjamin Rivlin (New York: Holmes & Meier Publishers, 1990), p. 14.

3. Urquhart, p. 179.

4. Ibid., p. 181.

5. Jim Haskins, *Ralph Bunche: A Most Reluctant Hero* (New York: Hawthorn Books, 1974), p. 65.

Chapter 2. The Long Journey West

1. Brian Urquhart, *Ralph Bunche: An American Life* (New York: W. W. Norton & Company, 1993), p. 25. Bunche's original birth certificate was lost, but his school records give his birth year as 1903. A note in the family Bible says 1904, and a new birth certificate issued in 1940 uses this date.

2. Ibid., p. 26.

3. Ibid., p. 27.

4. Ralph Bunche, "The Best Advice I Ever Had," *Reader's Digest*, March 1955, p. 133.

5. Ibid.

6. Urquhart, p. 28.

7. Ibid., p. 30.

8. Jim Haskins, *Ralph Bunche: A Most Reluctant Hero* (New York: Hawthorn Books, Inc., 1974), p. 92.

9. Ralph Bunche, "My Most Unforgettable Character," *Reader's Digest*, September 1969, p. 45.

10. Urquhart, p. 32.

11. John and Laree Caughey, *Los Angeles: Biography of a City* (Berkeley: University of California Press, 1976), p. 285.
12. Haskins, p. 30.

Chapter 3. Scholar-Athlete

1. Jim Haskins, *Ralph Bunche: A Most Reluctant Hero* (New York: Hawthorn Books, Inc., 1974), p. 34.
2. Ralph Bunche, "The Best Advice I Ever Had," *Reader's Digest*, March 1955, p. 133.
3. University of California at Los Angeles *Daily Bruin*, September 29, 1950, p. 1.
4. Brian Urquhart, *Ralph Bunche: An American Life* (New York: W. W. Norton & Company, 1993), p. 43.
5. Kenneth B. Clark, "Postscript: Ralph Bunche, the Human Being and the International Statesman," in *Ralph Bunche: The Man and His Times*, ed. Benjamin Rivlin (New York: Holmes & Meier Publishers, 1990), pp. 212–213.

Chapter 4. African Roots

1. Ralph Bunche, "The Thompson-Negro Alliance," in *Documentary History of the Negro People* (New York: Citadel Press, 1973), p. 624.
2. Nathan Irvin Huggins, "Ralph Bunche, the Africanist," in *Ralph Bunche: The Man and His Times*, ed. Benjamin Rivlin (New York: Holmes & Meier Publishers, 1990), p. 73.
3. John B. Kirby, "Race, Class, and Politics: Ralph Bunche and Black Protest," in Rivlin, *Ralph Bunche*, p. 35.
4. Ibid.
5. Charles P. Henry, "Civil Rights and National Security: The Case of Ralph Bunche," in Rivlin, *Ralph Bunche*, pp. 54–55.
6. Brian Urquhart, *Ralph Bunche: An American Life* (New York: W. W. Norton & Company, 1993), p. 63.
7. Ibid.
8. Ibid., p. 68.

9. Ralph J. Bunche, *An African American in South Africa: The Travel Notes of Ralph J. Bunche, 28 September 1937–1 January 1938* (Athens, Ohio: Ohio University Press, 1992), p. 25.

10. Ibid., p. 23.

11. Urquhart, p. 76.

Chapter 5. Sociology and War

1. Brian Urquhart, *Ralph Bunche: An American Life* (New York: W. W. Norton & Company, 1993), p. 81.

2. Dewey W. Grantham, *Political Status of the Negro in the Age of FDR* (Chicago: University of Chicago Press, 1973), p. xi.

3. Walter A. Jackson, *Gunnar Myrdal and America's Conscience* (Chapel Hill: University of North Carolina Press, 1990), p. 122.

4. Sissela Bok, *Alva Myrdal: A Daughter's Memoir,* Radcliff Biography Series (Reading, Mass.: Addison-Wesley Publishing Company, 1991), p. 84.

5. Benjamin Rivlin, "The Legacy of Ralph Bunche," in *Ralph Bunche: The Man and His Times*, ed. Benjamin Rivlin (New York: Holmes & Meier Publishers, 1990), p. 21.

6. Ibid.

7. Grantham, p. vii.

8. Jackson, pp. 319, 320.

9. Adolf Hitler, *Mein Kampf,* trans. by Ralph Manheim (Boston: Houghton Mifflin, 1943), pp. 383–393.

10. Ralph J. Bunche, *An African American in South Africa: The Travel Notes of Ralph J. Bunche, 28 September 1937–1 January 1938* (Athens, Ohio: Ohio University Press, 1992), p. 317.

11. Urquhart, p. 95.

12. Joseph P. Lash, *Eleanor: The Years Alone* (New York: W. W. Norton & Company, 1972), p. 249.

13. Ronald Takaki, *A Different Mirror: A History of Multicultural America* (Boston: Little, Brown & Co., 1993), p. 395.

14. Souad Halila, "The Intellectual Development and Diplomatic Career of Ralph J. Bunche" (Ph.D. diss., University of California, Los Angeles, May 1988), p. 112.

15. Bunche, p. 9.

16. Urquhart, p. 89.

17. Ibid., p. 109.

18. Kenneth B. Clark, "Postscript: Ralph Bunche, the Human Being and the International Statesman," in Rivlin, *Ralph Bunche*, p. 214.

Chapter 6. Peace at Last

1. Sanford S. Singer, "Ralph Bunche," in *The African American Encyclopedia* (New York: Michael Cavendish Corp., 1993), p. 242.

2. Brian Urquhart, *Ralph Bunche: An American Life* (New York: W. W. Norton & Company, 1993), p. 123.

3. Ibid., p. 131.

4. W. Ofuatey-Kodjoe, "Ralph Bunche: An African Perspective," in *Ralph Bunche: The Man and His Times*, ed. Benjamin Rivlin (New York: Holmes & Meier Publishers, 1990), p. 105.

5. Walter Laqueur and Barry Rubin, eds., *The Israeli-Arab Reader* (New York: Facts on File, Inc., 1985), pp. 108–110.

6. Record of the 365th Meeting of the Security Council, United Nations Official Records, Third Year, No. 116, October 14, 1948, pp. 17, 18.

7. Urquhart, p. 197.

Chapter 7. Nobel Laureate

1. J. C. Hurewitz, "Ralph Bunche as UN Acting Mediator: The Opening Phase," in *Ralph Bunche: The Man and His Times*, ed. Benjamin Rivlin (New York: Holmes & Meier Publishers, 1990), p. 175.

2. Ibid.

3. Shabtai Rosenne, "Bunche at Rhodes: Diplomatic Negotiator," in Rivlin, *Ralph Bunche*, p. 177.

4. Ibid., p. 185.

5. Sachar, p. 348.

6. Brian Urquhart, *Ralph Bunche: An American Life* (New York: W. W. Norton & Company, 1993), p. 211.

7. Ibid.

8. David Ben-Gurion, *Israel: A Personal History* (New York: Funk and Wagnalls, 1971), p. 318.

9. Moshe Dayan, *The Story of My Life* (New York: Plenum Publishing, 1992), p. 146.

10. Urquhart, p. 224.

11. J. Alvin Kugelmass, *Ralph Bunche: Fighter for Peace* (New York: Julian Messner, 1952), p. 143.

12. Urquhart, p. 231.

13. Benjamin Rivlin, "The Legacy of Ralph Bunche," in Rivlin, *Ralph Bunche*, p. 227.

14. Deborah Gillan Straub, ed., *Voices of Multicultural America* (Detroit: Gale Research, 1996), p. 109.

15. Ralph Bunche, *A World View of Race* (Washington, D.C.: Kennikat Press, Inc., 1936), p. 96.

16. Arthur M. Schlesinger, *Robert Kennedy and His Times,* vol. 1 (Boston: Houghton Mifflin, 1978), p. 89.

17. Straub, p. 116.

18. Ibid., p. 118.

19. John Hope Franklin, *From Slavery to Freedom: A History of Negro Americans* (New York: Alfred A. Knopf, 1967), p. 604.

Chapter 8. Congo Crisis

1. Brian Urquhart, *Ralph Bunche: An American Life* (New York: W. W. Norton & Company, 1993), p. 248.

2. Charles P. Henry, "Civil Rights and National Security: The Case of Ralph Bunche," in *Ralph Bunche: The Man and His Times*, ed. Benjamin Rivlin (New York: Holmes & Meier Publishers, 1990), p. 57.

3. Ralph J. Bunche, *An African American in South Africa: The Travel Notes of Ralph J. Bunche, 28 September 1937–1 January 1938* (Athens, Ohio: Ohio University Press, 1992), p. 7.

4. Alton Hornsby, ed., *African American Library* (Detroit: Gale Research, 1994), p. 106.

5. Dwight D. Eisenhower, *Waging Peace, 1956–1961* (Garden City, N.Y.: Doubleday & Company, 1965), p. 160.

6. Urquhart, p. 290.

7. Deborah Gillan Straub, ed., *Voices of Multicultural America* (Detroit: Gale Research, 1996), p. 122.

8. Ibid.

Chapter 9. Yemen, Cyprus, Vietnam

1. Brian Urquhart, *Ralph Bunche: An American Life* (New York: W. W. Norton & Company, 1993), p. 341.

2. U Thant, *View from the UN: The Memoirs of U Thant* (Garden City, N.Y.: Doubleday & Company, 1978), p. 113.

3. Benjamin Rivlin, "The Legacy of Ralph Bunche," in *Ralph Bunche: The Man and His Times*, ed. Benjamin Rivlin (New York: Holmes & Meier Publishers, 1990), p. 25.

4. Charles P. Henry, "Civil Rights and National Security: The Case of Ralph Bunche," in Rivlin, *Ralph Bunche*, p. 62.

5. Urquhart, p. 363.

6. Deborah Gillan Straub, ed., *Voices of Multicultural America* (Detroit: Gale Research, 1996), p. 122.

7. Ibid.

8. Urquhart, p. 367.

Chapter 10. Death of a Peacemaker

1. Brian Urquhart, *Ralph Bunche: An American Life* (New York: W. W. Norton & Company, 1993), p. 380.

2. U Thant, *View From the UN: The Memoirs of U Thant* (Garden City, N.Y.: Doubleday & Company, 1978), p. 58.

3. Ibid., p. 63.

4. Ralph Bunche, "On Race: The Alienation of Modern Man," in *Ralph Bunche, The Man and His Times*, ed. Benjamin Rivlin (New York: Holmes & Meier Publishers, 1990), p. 264.

5. Urquhart, p. 394.

6. Ibid., p. 391.

7. Thant, p. 50.

8. Benjamin Rivlin, introduction to Rivlin, *Ralph Bunche*, p. xiii.

9. Ibid.

10. Ibid., p. 5.

11. Ibid., p. 22.

12. Alton Hornsby, ed., *African American Library* (Detroit: Gale Research, 1994), p. 106.

13. "A Tribute to a Disciple of Peace," *United Nations Bulletin*, October 1, 1949, pp. 411, 412.

FURTHER READING

Bunche, Ralph J. *An African American in South Africa: The Travel Notes of Ralph J. Bunche, 28 September 1937–1 January 1938.* Athens, Ohio: Ohio University Press, 1992.

Haskins, Jim. *Ralph Bunche: A Most Reluctant Hero.* New York: Hawthorn Books, 1974.

Kugelmass, J. Alvin. *Ralph Bunche: Fighter for Peace.* New York: Julian Messner, 1952.

Laqueur, Walter, and Barry Rubin, eds. *The Israeli-Arab Reader.* New York: Facts on File, Inc., 1985.

McKissack, Patricia, and Fredrick McKissack. *Ralph J. Bunche: Peacemaker.* Hillside, N.J.: Enslow Publishers, Inc., 1991.

Rivlin, Benjamin, ed. *Ralph Bunche: The Man and His Times.* New York: Holmes & Meier Publishers, 1990.

Stein, R. Conrad. *The United Nations.* Danbury, Conn.: Children's Press, 1994.

Urquhart, Brian. *Ralph Bunche: An American Life.* New York: W. W. Norton & Company, 1993.

Internet Addresses

http://nobelprizes.com/nobel/peace/1950a.html

http://library.advanced.org/10320/Bunche.htm

http://www.kaiwan.com/~mcivr/bunche.html

INDEX